# The Price Guide to
# Victorian, Edwardian and 1920s Furniture

## (1860-1930)

## John Andrews

*Antique Collectors' Club*

© copyright 1980    John Andrews
Reprinted 1981

World copyright reserved
ISBN 0 902028 89 8

British Library CIP Data
Andrews, John
    The Price Guide to Victorian and
    Edwardian Furniture
    1. Furniture, Victorian — England —
    Collectors and collecting
    2. Furniture, Edwardian — England —
    Collectors and collecting
    I. Title II. Antique Collectors' Club Ltd.
    749.2'2    NK2530

    ISBN 0 902028 89 8

Published for the Antique Collectors' Club
by the Antique Collectors' Club Ltd.

Printed in England by
Baron Publishing, Woodbridge, Suffolk

*Why not join —*

# *The Antique Collectors' Club*

The Antique Collectors' Club was formed in 1966 and now has a five figure membership spread throughout the world. It publishes the only independently run monthly antiques magazine *Antique Collecting* which caters for those collectors who are interested in increasing their knowledge of antiques, both by increasing the members' knowledge of quality as well as in discussing the factors which influence the price that is likely to be asked. The Antique Collectors' Club pioneered the provision of information on prices for collectors and still leads in the provision of detailed articles on a variety of subjects.

It was in response to the enormous demand for information on "what to pay" that the price guide series was introduced in 1968 with the first edition of *The Price Guide to Antique Furniture* also by John Andrews, which was completely revised in 1978. The book broke new ground by illustrating the more common types of antique furniture, the sort that collectors could buy in shops and at auctions, rather than the rare museum pieces which had previously been used (and still to a large extent are used) to make up the limited amount of illustrations in books published by commercial publishers. Many other price guides have followed, all copiously illustrated, and greatly appreciated by collectors for the valuable information they contain, quite apart from prices. The Antique Collectors Club also publishes other books on antiques, including horology and art reference works, and a full book list is available.

Club membership, which is open to all collectors, costs £8.95 per annum. Members receive free of charge *Antique Collecting,* the Club's magazine (published every month except August), which contains well-illustrated articles dealing with the practical aspects of collecting not normally dealt with by magazines. Prices, features of value, investment potential, fakes and forgeries are all given prominence in the magazine.

Among other facilities available to members are private buying and selling facilities, the longest list of "For Sales" of any antiques magazine, an annual ceramics conference and the opportunity to meet other collectors at their local antique collectors' club. There are nearly eighty in Britain and so far a dozen overseas. Members may also buy the Club's publications at special pre-publication prices.

As its motto implies, the Club is an amateur organisation designed to help collectors to get the most out of their hobby: it is informal and friendly and gives enormous enjoyment to all concerned.

*For Collectors  —  By Collectors  —  About Collecting*

**The Antique Collectors' Club, 5 Church Street, Woodbridge, Suffolk**

## PRICE REVISION LISTS

### January Annually

### (The first to be published January 1982)

As collectors are well aware, the value of furniture changes with the result that the values shown in this book will gradually become outdated.

It is reasonable to anticipate that over a period of several years the price of old furniture will rise but by no means all pieces rise at the same rate.

In order to keep the prices in this book fully up to date, a Price Revision List is published annually. This is available during January at a cost of £1.67 by banker's order or £1.85 cash. A banker's order is enclosed with this book.

**Antique Collectors' Club**
**5 Church Street, Woodbridge, Suffolk**

# Contents

|  | page |
|---|---|
| **Acknowledgements** | 9 |
| **Photographic Acknowledgements** | 10 |
| **Furniture Prices** | 11 |
| **British Furniture Styles 1860-1930** | 13-42 |
| Victorian rococo 1830-1890 | 16 |
| Elizabethan (including Jacobean and Stuart) 1830-1890 | 17 |
| 18th century reproductions and derivations | 18 |
| Gothic and the Reformers | 20 |
| Art Furniture — the Aesthetic Movement, 1865-1890 | 26 |
| Anglo-Japanese, 1865-1890 | 27 |
| the Arts and Crafts Movement | 29 |
| the Nineteen Twenties, 1918-1930 | 35 |
| **Bureau Bookcases** | 43-47 |
| elongated Edwardian | 46 |
| **Bureaux** | 48-57 |
| bonheurs-du-jour | 48 |
| cylinder front | 49 |
| elongated Edwardian | 50 |
| reproduction | 52-57 |
| *on bracket feet* | 52 |
| *on legs* | 55 |
| **Cabinets** | 58-77 |
| bookcases | 58-63 |
| *high* | 58 |
| *low* | 62 |
| *revolving* | 63 |
| side, credenzas | 64 |
| side and display | 66-75 |
| *1860-1890* | 66 |
| *'art nouveau' 1890-1910* | 68 |
| *1890-1930* | 70 |
| *'Louis' monstrosities, 1900-1914* | 71 |
| *reproductions 1880-1930, high* | 72 |
| *reproductions 1880-1930, lower* | 75 |
| side, court cupboards, buffets and the like | 77 |
| **Canterburies** | 78 |
| **Chairs** | 79-114 |
| bentwood | 79 |
| balloon back, Victorian | 80 |
| straight front legs, Victorian | 81 |
| reproductions, 1880-1930 | 83 |
| small Edwardian oak | 88 |
| Arts and Crafts, Art Nouveau and after: 1860-1930 | 90 |
| country and kitchen | 95-100 |
| *rush-seated, 1860-1930* | 95 |
| *wooden seated, 1860-1930* | 98 |
| rocking and special purpose | 101 |
| corner | 102 |
| upholstered | 103-114 |
| *Victorian spoon backs* | 103 |
| *Victorian uprights* | 104 |
| *'designers' chairs, 1860-1910* | 106 |
| *occasional* | 108 |
| *reproductions* | 111 |
| *arm and easy, 1890-1930* | 112 |

*Contents continued*

|  |  | page |
|---|---|---|
| **Chests** | | 115-125 |
| coffers | | 115 |
| of drawers — 1860-1930 | | 117 |
| dressing | | 122 |
| military | | 124 |
| Wellington and specimen | | 125 |
| **Desks** | | 126-135 |
| davenports | | 126 |
| pedestal | | 128 |
| roll-top | | 132 |
| Wootton Patent Office | | 134 |
| **Dressers** | | 136-140 |
| **Mirrors** | | 141-145 |
| wall and pier, including girandoles | | 141 |
| cheval | | 144 |
| dressing | | 145 |
| **Pine Furniture** | | 146-149 |
| **Pot Cupboards** | | 150 |
| **Settees, Chaises-longues and Sofas** | | 151-157 |
| chaises-longues | | 151 |
| chesterfields | | 153 |
| art nouveau | | 154 |
| drop arm | | 154 |
| 'reproduction' styles, 1890-1930 | | 155 |
| **Settles** | | 158-159 |
| **Sideboards** | | 160-177 |
| 1860-1900 | | 160 |
| 1900-1920 | | 164 |
| art nouveau and progressive, 1890-1915 | | 166 |
| reproduction, 1880-1930 | | 168-173 |
| *18th and early 19th century mahogany* | | 168 |
| *'Queen Anne' leading to 'burr walnut bedappled'* | | 170 |
| *'Jacobean' oak varieties* | | 172 |
| chiffoniers | | 174 |
| hybrid, 1900-1930 | | 175 |
| 'modern', 1920-1930 | | 176 |
| **Stands** | | 178-180 |
| hall | | 178 |
| occasional | | 180 |
| **Stools** | | 181 |
| **Tables** | | 182-208 |
| centre pedestal | | 182-184 |
| *Gothic* | | 184 |
| dining | | 185-189 |
| *on four legs* | | 185 |
| *oak reproductions* | | 188 |
| dressing | | 190 |
| gateleg | | 195 |
| occasional | | 197-200 |
| *centre* | | 197 |
| *tripod* | | 200 |
| side and card | | 201 |
| Sutherland | | 205 |
| work and games | | 206 |
| writing | | 207 |
| **Wardrobes** | | 209-214 |
| **Washstands** | | 215-216 |
| **Bibliography** | | 217 |

# Acknowledgements

This book is, as always, a team effort and I would like to acknowledge and thank the following people who have played major roles in its production:—

**My wife, Geraldine**    without whom nothing would get written and whose natural artistic affinity for the period of 1880 to 1930 has helped me to understand many aspects.

**My son, Sam**    who interrupted a budding literary activity to help produce another of what he describes as my 'catalogues'.

**Christopher Payne**    furniture expert of Sotheby's Belgravia, who gave great assistance with the whole period generally and who allowed access to the many fine illustrations used.

**Susanne Elphick**    also of Sotheby's Belgravia, whose real practical assistance with illustrations saved much time and effort.

**Pauline Agius**    for stimulating discussion of the period and whose book on British Furniture provided much essential information.

**Michael Whiteway**    art dealer, of Haslam & Whiteway, London, a specialist in the architect-designers, who generously overcame his natural detestation of price guides and provided valuable illustrations, discussion and information.

**John Steel**    publisher, who as always, acted as my other half and sounding-board in conceiving this book as well as providing much constructive criticism and assistance with the text.

**Diana Steel**    printer and publisher, who, with her staff, actually does the real work and makes the final product look much better than I can conceive it.

In writing a book on this period the author lays himself open to being torpedoed by many a submarine art researcher and historian, let alone the antique trade itself. Any corrections, additions and factually-based amendments would be gratefully received and humbly acknowledged in future editions.

# Photographic Acknowledgements

The author and publishers are deeply grateful to the following who either took or allowed photographs to be taken of the items used in this book:—

**The Antique Furniture Warehouse, Woodbridge, Suffolk**
**Bonhams, London**
**Christie's, London**
**Jeremy Cooper Ltd., Galen Place, London**
**The Fine Art Society, Bond Street, London**
**The Old Mint House, Pevensey, Sussex**
**John Phelps of Phelps Ltd., Twickenham**
**The Pine Mine, Wandsworth Bridge Road, London**
**Alan Shead, Rose Cottage Antiques, Knox Bridge, Staplehurst, Kent**
**Silvester's of Warwick**
**Sotheby's Belgravia, London**
**The Victoria and Albert Museum**
**Michael Whiteway of Haslam & Whiteway Ltd., Kensington Church Street, London**

# Furniture Prices 1860~1930
# A Reprise

In the preparation of this book, doubts were expressed by some distinguished contributors as to the possibility of recording any useful values where the finest pieces, attributable to the most famous designers and craftsmen, were concerned. Since such pieces are frequently sought by museums rather than by collectors or the general public, the market that exists for them does not fall into a predictable range.

Much the same misgivings were expressed when the *Price Guide to Antique Furniture,* covering the years 1660-1860, was produced in 1969 and again, in revised form, in 1978. These same doubts were, however, successfully dispelled by the application of a basic principle that is equally applicable to the furniture covered by this volume as it is to that of the earlier period.

It is an interesting concept that the architect-designed furniture of the late 19th and early 20th century has moved out of the scale of values to be expected for furniture and into that normally applicable to Art. The work of any designer who is in the sequential line leading to the Modern Movement, such as Mackintosh, commands prices which are way out of scale with those applicable to high-quality furniture. Painted furniture by Seddon and Burges, on another plane, is similarly treated as Art. Whether it conforms to the basic principles of good design in regard to function — fitness for the purpose — or of limitation of embellishment, seems to be irrelevant, because Mackintosh's furniture often fails the first test and Seddon/Burges the second. The pieces are being treated as Works of Art rather than as furniture and hence the prices go into orbit.

The fact is that a piece of furniture attributable to a great name, whether it be Adam, Chippendale, or Hepplewhite, as examples of the 18th century, or Pugin, Burges, Voysey or Mackintosh for the 19th, immediately must be regarded as outside the scope of a book intended to show the broad range of widely-available furniture in the general run of antique and junk shops. In such cases, the only indication that can be given is either a minimum value below which it can be said with near certainty that the piece will not be available, or to show an auction value, such as the £90,000 recently paid for a cabinet by Mackintosh. Both have their drawbacks since special considerations apply to each piece in question but they establish, nevertheless, a basic point of reference.

The point of principle that the author and publishers most strongly wish to make is that to produce a book like this without including such pieces would render it valueless, almost useless as a guide. For the ordinary collector to understand the reasons for the values of the run-of-the-mill furniture available, he or she needs to be aware of the aims of the top-level designers and craftsmen and to see how these aims affected the design and production of commercial furniture. For this reason we have continued the concept of showing grades of quality and/or derivations of design from the highest to the lowest, where possible. Only in this way can a broad view of where the scales of values should fall be obtained. There is, of course, the additional benefit to the reader that he or she might one day fall over a piece that closely resembles the finest or most expensive works illustrated and be advised accordingly.

For the unattributable, normally-available furniture shown in this book the same market research and principles on the scale of values shown is used as that now successfully used in all the Price Guide series and, in particular, the *Price Guide to Antique Furniture* (second edition). The price ranges shown represent the prices at which the pieces may be purchased by a collector willing to make a little effort to go out and find the pieces illustrated. If a specialist dealer is approached for a particular piece, then clearly some premium must be paid for his time, effort, knowledge and financing of the stock necessary. If a specialist auction is used for a particular piece or because of limitation of time available, then, again, some premium may have to be paid due to competition from a similarly-placed rival. It is an irony of today's trading conditions that, very often, higher prices are paid at auction for pieces available in nearby dealers' shops and yet dealers buy a great deal at auction.

# British Furniture Styles 1860-1930

## An Overview, with the benefit of Hindsight

To many people, the furniture styles of the period from 1860 to 1930 are horrifyingly confusing. Until quite recently they were regarded with loathing by 'People of Taste'. Some pieces present a stylistic collage, in which features from many periods clash with each other. Some pieces are clearly simpler, but derivative from earlier periods. There are clearly identifiable types, such as rococo or Gothic, and there are reproductions of Sheraton, Chippendale, Queen Anne and Adam. There is much bogus oak.

It is not only the styles which confuse. The terminology can be worse. Why is 'art furniture' nothing like art nouveau? Why did the Arts and Crafts Movement, some of whose associates are said to have inspired art nouveau, disapprove very strongly of art nouveau as a degenerate Continental form, whose sinuous plasticity was against their principles? And there are too many names to remember for an 18th century buff (who can get by with about three): Morris, Burges, Godwin, Voysey, and those similar-sounding Scots' names like Mackmurdo and Mackintosh, to mention only a few. It is all too difficult. There is so much of it to remember and the experts are often confusing, for it is a period which attracts the art student, the architect and the intellectual rather than the plain honest furniture man.

The illustrated pages which follow outline the major popular styles where they can be separately identified and the work of the reforming designers who became so influential as the period progressed. They have been arranged so as to demonstrate the great division in Victorian furniture design caused by the conflict between tradition and reform. It was a conflict that ran through all the culture of the period, including art and literature. Nowhere was it stronger than in furniture. From 1835 to 1860 it was mainly factory-produced furniture that satisfied the tastes of the majority and these tastes were based on traditional or past styles, used in somewhat free-handed forms, provided they were not 18th century in character, since there was an intense hatred of 18th century furniture which lasted until the 1860s.

All this did not suddenly change in 1860, the starting date of this book. Up to then the traditionalists had had it pretty much their own way and they continued to produce these past styles in great quantity, turning to 18th century styles of Adam, Queen Anne, Chippendale, Hepplewhite and Sheraton as the '60s and '70s went on. But in 1861 the firm of William Morris & Co. was founded. Morris was not the first of the reformers; Pugin is generally credited with that accolade, based on his *Gothic Furniture* of 1835, which had little immediate effect but which inspired many imitators by the 1850s. In fact, at the Great Exhibition of 1851, he organised the Medieval Court, which was widely discussed. These Gothic forms, with Ruskin's inspiration as well, attracted the attention of a new wave of architect-designers such as Seddon, Webb, Burges and Shaw, so that the London International Exhibition of 1862 marks the point at which 'Reformers' Gothic' came strongly before the public. William Morris exhibited pieces designed by Seddon and Webb at this exhibition, which also featured work by Burges and Shaw. The 1860s became a great era of Gothic revival.

There were thus two broad categories of British furniture in existence from 1860 onwards. The first, numerically greatest, was the mass-produced and craftsman's furniture made in antiquarian styles. The second was a series of Reformers' or Progressive designs which gradually became more influential and which came to be copied by commercial firms by the 1880s and 1890s. These progressive designs in their turn included Anglo-Japanese and art nouveau furniture. The trouble with the reformers was that many of them — Morris and Gimson are classic examples — simply could not come to terms with machines or, in Morris's case, could not afford them. They turned back, Luddite-like, towards the artist-craftsman concept in a purely handcraft sense, without realising what the machine could have done for them. Thus they often did fine work but remained makers of individual pieces rather than taking on the task of making well-designed furniture available for a much wider range of homes. What is more, their love of the medieval and the appreciation they engendered for it led to the rise of an awful new activity: antique collecting and reproductions. By 1900 a vogue for old oak furniture had become widely spread and, with it, a sort of eclectic 'Olde Englishe' bogusness that led eventually to the Tudor-style estates of houses built in the 1920s and 1930s, containing 'Jacobean' style dining rooms almost *de rigueur*.

But we should not neglect the fact that Morris and his disciples stimulated public awareness, even though Morris was not greatly interested in furniture and concentrated upon textiles and wallpaper, apart from poetry and prose. The designers who Morris inspired — Gimson and the Barnsleys, Lethaby, Blomfield and others of Kenton & Co., the Artworkers' Guild, the Arts and Crafts Exhibition Society and others — detailed in subsequent pages — awakened many people to the need for clean simple furniture of good design. Ambrose Heal, Liberty and other large London stores fostered machine-made furniture which stood up to the test, so that by 1914 it was not only the isolated craftsmen who were standing out against a flood of trade-built reproductions and ghastly fussiness.

Two other designers deserve separate mention. C.F.A. Voysey and C.R. Mackintosh are independent designers whose work had enormous influence, particularly on the Continent. From the 1880s to 1914 they produced designs which gave rise to furniture of really original shapes which came to be widely copied by the commercial trade, much of it being what would now loosely be called art nouveau. (Arthur Heygate Mackmurdo, mentioned earlier, was another textile/wallpaper designing architect who also designed the first English 'sinuous' furniture, was a friend of Morris's and, like him, was concerned with craftsmanship and design.)

After the First World War there was an incredible void. The fashions of pre-1914 were dead. Art nouveau was right out. Mackintosh eventually went to the South of France to paint watercolours, eking out a living on his savings and his wife's small private income. Voysey was virtually unemployed. The spirit of originality seems to have disappeared. Reproductions and derivations carried on, sustained by momentum rather than force. The easiest thing was to rely on the 18th century. At the same time, the lack of domestic servants led to a sort of 'cottage-socialist' school, obsessed with clean, cheap surfaces needing a minimum of dusting. Perhaps the most interesting example of the dilemma facing that school — acceptance of the existing taste combined with advocacy of garden suburb sterility — can be seen in the published work of Percy Wells, a fine craftsman and head of the cabinet department of the Shoreditch Technical Institute, in the heart of what was once London's furniture manufacturing area.

Wells produced, with John Hooper of the City and Guilds Institute, *Modern Cabinet Work,* initially in 1909, but revising it in 1911, 1918, 1922 and 1924. It is full of examples of how to produce the finest reproduction cabinet work — Buhl, William and Mary, Sheraton, Adam, Chippendale and Hepplewhite. It also illustrates work by Gimson, J.S. Henry, Morris, Heal and Gordon Russell. But in 1920, Percy Wells produced *Furniture for Small Houses.* In it he advocates 'plain furniture' — some of it almost Spartan in its depressing plainness. He is obsessed with dusting, economy and inexpensiveness, hates 'flashy and flimsy' modern furniture, rails against 'embellishments and meritricious ornament' for which 'middle class people blindly pay high prices'. Even accepting that he was writing for those to whom economy was important, the imposition of a sterilised atmosphere is not conducive to domestic repose. Some of the furniture of Percy Wells and 1920s' designers of this type is greatly to be admired for simplicity and fine line. Some of it has an institutional thriftiness, a sort of sanatorium quality that genuflects towards the greyness of a totalitarian state.

In 1925 the Salon des Arts Décoratifs was held in France and gave the title, in shortened form, to art deco, which is used now to describe furniture and design of a certain kind. In fact the beginnings of art deco go back before this convenient date, much as the designs of Chippendale can be found before the publication of his *Director* in 1755. It is a loose appellation, generally covering furniture of the later 1920s and 1930s with certain motifs like the sunburst, zig-zags and curved edges without mouldings. When David Joel wrote his book on *British Furniture* in 1953, he used the term 'Jazz Age' to describe some furniture he detested. This is now sold as art deco. It is too early, and we are probably too close, to determine what is currently merely fashionable and what will endure from this period, for much of it is flashy and flimsy. But then, so was some of Mackintosh's work, so who are we to say?

The period covered by this book is one of enormous furniture output and variety of style. Its central span, 1890-1910, marks the zenith of British power, wealth and confidence. The arts flourish in such an atmosphere and it will be possible to obtain much more detailed research on this period than earlier ones. Much remains to be discovered and designers to be identified. Many pieces have disappeared — indeed one of the features of the currently-famous designers' work is that there is so little of it. There were many producers who claimed themselves to be islands of good taste in a sea of shoddiness. But remember: through it all, above the deafening bellows of the reformers, the shrieks of the arty-crafty and the squeals of the fashionable (like the voice of Sir Thomas Picton at the storming of Badajoz "consigning everyone to eternal damnation") the furniture trade continued to turn out the reproduction, the copy and the just plain comfortable for the mass of people who wanted it.

# Furniture Styles

## Victorian Rococo 1830-1890

One of the most enduring styles of the Victorian period was the rococo furniture which Victorians referred to as Louis XIV, but which was, in fact, more correctly Louis XV. It first appeared as a reaction to the rather severe and sometimes dull sub-classical designs of the Regency and William IV periods — those Greek, Gothic, French Empire-Egyptian, Elizabethan and other rather historic styles that possibly invoked a feeling of duty to taste rather than pleasure in their beholders.

Rococo can be traced back as far as the early 1820s but it probably was in full swing in the 1840s and through the 1850s. What made it so enduringly popular was probably its highly decorative nature. Trade catalogues of the 1880s and even the 1890s still illustrated it, although by then it was no longer widely popular. The later rococo furniture of the 19th century — perhaps from the 1860s onwards — tends to lose the flowing, assured lines of the earlier period. The odd cusp or point suddenly cranks a curve and there is, quite often, a dot-dash grooving to interrupt the surface. Despite the destruction of much of it, from the 1920s onwards until it came back into antique fashion in the early 1960s, large quantities have survived, so it must really have caught on. Handley-Read points out that it was frivolous and hence a decorator's style, whereas architects frowned upon it. This is perhaps one of the key points to bear in mind about the period, since little of the architects furniture is to be seen now.

*The rococo, as applied to chairs, generally affected the legs and arms but in this bergère chair of the 1850s-1860s has also gone into the scrolling of the top rail. Such chairs were still made and shown in manufacturers' catalogues of the 1880s, although the style was out of date by then.*

*A walnut centre table of c.1860, showing how the scrolls and swerves of the rococo 'Louis XIVth' style were applied to the rather decorative and exuberant mid-Victorian period.*

*The rococo as applied to a fire screen with needle-work tapestry. Note the extensively scrolled rosewood frame and the use of the acanthus leaf in carving — a classic Victorian decoration.*

## Elizabethan (including Jacobean and Stuart) 1830-1890

One of the popular styles of the late Regency — possibly inspired by Walter Scott's novels — which continued well into the Victorian period. Scott's house, Abbotsford, enlarged after 1819, became a famous example of the Scottish Baronial — Hollywood style and certain pieces of furniture have acquired the Abbotsford adjective as typical of the genre.

In fact, Victorian Elizabethan furniture leans upon Tudor, Jacobean and Stuart styles. It is not averse to leaning upon a few others, either. The twist-turned, or barley-sugar column, leg, upright and stretcher is a feature of this 'Elizabethan' furniture, but not always. Sometimes cabriole legs borrowed from the rococo might also be included.

Carolean chairs of the caned type and Restoration Stuart furniture seem to have had a very popular vogue towards the end of the century, particularly the 1890s, when antique collecting and reproductions of 18th century styles also were in fashion. These Stuart chairs must have been turned out in large numbers, since there are plenty of them still in evidence, and must have gone well with the 'Jacobean' and 'early English oak' dining rooms that were by then so popular.

*A first-class example of a mixture of styles. The back of this mahogany low chair is in what the Victorians called the 'Elizabethan' manner, with twist-turned uprights — actually belonging to the Restoration (1660) rather than the Elizabethan (1558-1603) period. The legs, however, owe nothing to the style of the back and are typical early Victorian cabrioles following the Louis XV or French Rococo (misnamed Louis XIV by the Victorians) style then popular.*

*Three prie-dieu chairs with Berlin woodwork coverings from Cheval & Pole Screens, Ottomans etc., by Henry Wood, published c.1850. All three show the influence of the 'Elizabethan' style, but particularly the two outer chairs with their twist-turned uprights and finials.*

*(Left) Another example of the Victorian 'Elizabethan' style in a rosewood chair with woolwork upholstery. The twist-turning of the back uprights is capped by the very typical turned finials of the 1850s and 1860s and there are 'C' scrolls embellishing the centre splat. The legs and stretchers are turned in a later Stuart baluster style.*

*(Right) An oak dining carver chair typical of the late 19th century 'Jacobean' type, harking back to the 'Elizabethan' taste of the early part of the century. Twist-turning is used more consistently but the style leans more on Restoration Stuart forms than anything else.*

# 18th Century Reproductions and Derivations 1860-present day

*A late Victorian 'Chippendale' chair in mahogany, on cabriole legs ending in ball-and-claw feet. The back uses a Gothic design form in the splat but the wavy uprights are not to period and the ankles of the cabrioles show typical Victorian weakness.*

*(Adam, Chippendale, Hepplewhite, Queen Anne and Sheraton — to name but a few, in alphabetical order)*

To anyone engaged in collecting 18th century furniture in the 1980s, the furniture made from the late 1860s onwards is a frightening prospect. Until the 1860s, the Victorians wished to forget 18th century styles but, almost as a logical result of their 'education' by Morris and the reformers, they were bound to come round, or back, to these styles as their appreciation of cleaner lines and purer original tastes was developed. In some senses, the early Victorians, despite their prejudices, had not deserted some of the 18th century sources anyway. Adam is a classical style; rococo was used by Chippendale; Hepplewhite and Sheraton are French-influenced. But in the 1870s and 1880s it appears to have become increasingly acceptable to go back to the 18th century in a purely copying sense and to attempt, not a Victorian 'version' of the other styles they had developed, but a real copy of the original.

Many of these copies are, quite clearly, wrong in proportion, design or execution, or all three. *The Price Guide to Antique Furniture* shows examples of how these mass-produced copies were wrong. There were, however, firms of excellent craftsmen who produced versions of 18th century furniture that were remarkable in spirit, interpretation and skill, using materials of the highest quality. The firm of Wright & Mansfield is often cited as the instigator of the revival and, in particular, their neo-classical Adam-style cabinet exhibited at the 1867 Exhibition in Paris, although they also exhibited neo-classical 18th century detail in 1862 in London. But the Wright & Mansfield cabinet of 1867 is not likely to disturb very much the modern-day collector of antiques. It is the pieces made from the 1870s onwards by them and by superb firms like Edwards & Roberts (usually identifiable from makers' labels) which are now so difficult to distinguish from the originals. Many faithful copies must have been made for country and town house owners to replace damaged items, to increase the numbers in sets of chairs, or simply to duplicate for a variety of reasons. There was also, however, a thriving trade in fakes and in the 'improvement' of workaday furniture of earlier periods, by carving or by adding decorative inlays and crossbandings to plain surfaces. Sometimes these activities are evident from the character of the piece, but some of the less forthright cabinet makers and firms were in the business of making 'antiques' and had no scruples about passing off their work as something much older. It is highly probable that many pieces now sold as 18th century antiques originated in this way.

The Victorians were rather vague themselves about stylistic attribution and used the term Queen Anne, or Chippendale and other 18th century names, to describe pieces which were only vaguely related to the original style. We have not bothered here to plot the course of such mistaken appellations, preferring to deal with the pieces on the basis of present-day knowledge.

*Another Victorian 'Chippendale' chair of simpler form using a 'country Chippendale' back and rather shortened arms. The square tapering legs belong more to Sheraton style and look weak in balance with back; the original straight square legs of the 18th century would have looked better.*

(Right) A composite piece made c.1920 with a Dutch-Queen Anne glazed display cabinet on top of a base which uses 'Queen Anne' cabriole legs connected by a curvy Sheraton stretcher system with central platform (presumably for a vase or other display piece). The drawers are embellished with mouldings of a French rococo nature.

A mahogany bureau bookcase of 'Sheraton' style with a broken pediment but in fact made around 1900. It has the inlaid Adam-Sheraton swags of classical derivation on the fall — a motif very popular in the 1890-1910 period. Note also the satinwood banding to the drawers, beloved of Edwardian Sheratonians.

(Right) A mahogany sideboard or side cabinet made 1910-1920 in an 18th century style based on Chippendale designs. Although of good quality workmanship, it is clumsier than a period piece would be; the heavy square feet do not help.

A corner cupboard in the Gothic Revival manner, showing the pointed arches typical of the style. It also has carved decoration which includes the whorls, suns, 'pies', sunflowers and other motifs of the 1860s Revivalist designers.

(Below left) A Puginian type of centre table showing characteristics of the earlier type of Gothic Revival furniture — architectural in concept and decoration and superbly made. 1850-1860.

(Below right) A table by Pugin in the Gothic Revival style c.1851 in which ogee curves are used extensively in the very structural base.

# Gothic and the Reformers — Revivalist Gothic 1860-1890

| | | |
|---|---|---|
| W. Burges | W. Morris & Co. | R. Norman Shaw |
| E. Burne-Jones | A.W.N. Pugin | B. Talbert |
| C.L. Eastlake | J.P. Seddon | P. Webb |

The origins of the Gothic style are said to be Islamic, since the pointed arch is a feature of that culture. The Normans are said to have found it in Sicily and hence brought it to England where, from about the year 1200, an indigenous version was developed and used for several centuries. Chippendale used the style in the 18th century and so did the designers of the Regency period in the early 19th century in rather decorated form. It is A.W. Pugin who, in 1835, published his *Gothic Furniture* and set off the reform in design away from the sub-classical sources used in the 1830s and 1840s. In all senses, he marked the watershed between the 'Gothick' used by the Regency designers, the early Victorian Gothic of the '40s and '50s, and the reformed or revivalist Gothic of the '60s and onwards, since he provides examples of all three types.

After the Great Exhibition of 1851, at which Pugin's Medieval Court caused wide discussion, Ruskin in 1853 published his *Stones of Venice* in which a chapter 'The Nature of Gothic' was a source of inspiration to the reformers. William Morris, using the designers Webb and Seddon, exhibited at the 1862 London International Exhibition, at which Norman Shaw and William Burges also showed Gothic furniture. All of them were supposedly reacting aginst the over-ornamental furniture of their time but their exhibition pieces were conceived on a rather massive scale, inflated to vastly out-of-domestic proportions. What is more, these exhibition pieces were highly decorated — the Morris cabinets were extensively painted by Morris himself, Madox Brown, Rossetti and Burne-Jones, so that in one sense they were no different from the commercial and popular pieces with which they were exhibited. Indeed, in these pieces of Morris's, in which the plain wood surface is hardly allowed to appear, it is difficult to conceive of the furniture with which one associates the company and which was subsequently made by them.

Little of Norman Shaw's subsequent work has been found. Burges continued to design furniture in the Gothic style, much of it quite elaborate, until his death in 1881. Seddon produced books of drawings of Gothic furniture but only the 1862 exhibition pieces are known of his work. Webb continued with William Morris & Co.

*A much simpler table showing a version of Pugin forms but far straighter in style as might be expected from later derivations. Possibly 1860s.*

## A.W. Pugin, 1812-1852

All the early reformers or 'progressive' designers acknowledged their debt to Pugin. His theoretical version of Gothic (not the picturesque, decorative 'Gothick' of the Regency, which his father had illustrated in 1820 and which Loudon showed in 1833) was concerned with revealed construction and lack of sham decoration, a sort of solid, simple version with plain arched construction. In practice, he had designed the decorative kind as a young man for Windsor Castle and his work includes some very unreformed Gothic examples. Nonetheless, his simpler designs were probably popular and were copied by commercial producers.

## William Morris & Co.

As we have said earlier, Morris himself was not greatly interested in furniture — his early attempts were over heavy, structurally unsound and disastrously large — so that the firm's furniture tended to be left to the chief designers. Among these were Philip Webb, George Jack and William Lethaby, who designed furniture that was not necessarily always different from that of other good commercial producers. They often used simple traditional designs; the rush-seated Sussex chairs are an example. They made reproduction-inspired satinwood furniture in the 1890s and 1900s; they made both cheap and expensive furniture; they made green stained bedroom furniture from a jollop introduced by Ford Madox Brown in the 1860s. In other words, Morris & Co. were a good-quality commercial firm whose furniture is often difficult to date and who moved with the times. It is a relief that they did and that Morris, in this sense, was otherwise occupied, for one cannot help feeling uneasy about a man, however industrious and influential, who half-aimed at the Church, was financially independent, formed undergraduate-style brotherhoods, buried his head in medievalism at a time of vibrant industrial and Imperial thrust, and took to Icelandic sagas and socialism to obliterate the hurtful association of his wife with the distasteful Rossetti; an association brought about by the idealised worship of women as distant, ethereal creatures which he and Burne-Jones shared. William Morris & Co. are referred to again under Arts and Crafts Movement (see page 31).

*The William Morris-Seddon version of 1862 Gothic, exhibited at the London Exhibition. In oak, with panels painted by Madox Brown, Burne-Jones, Rossetti and Morris on a design of cabinet by the architect J.P. Seddon. Never intended as domestic furniture and made to make statements about design.*

### Edward Burne-Jones, 1833-1898

Plays but a glancing role in this volume, confined to some of the painted decoration on the Brobdignagian Morris furniture exhibited at the 1862 Exhibition. One of the most highly regarded artists of the Victorian era, Burne-Jones was essentially a religious artist who also fell in with the Morrisian nonsense of Arthurian legend and weepy angelic figures. Although a major figure in British art, the lack of virility of many of his figures makes one sympathise with the scathing remark of John Bidlake, the Augustus-John fictional painter in Aldous Huxley's *Point Counterpoint:* "The man painted as though he had never seen a pair of buttocks in his life."

### John Pollard Seddon, 1827-1906

Designed furniture for Morris & Co. at the 1862 Exhibition. A roll-top desk with much decoration designed by him and made by Thomas Seddon is shown here. J.P. Seddon left several books of designs for Gothic furniture (now in the Victoria and Albert Museum). Little has been identified of his work apart from the 'King Rene's Honeymoon Cabinet' also shown at the 1862 Exhibition.

### Philip Webb, 1831-1915

Architect, met William Morris in the office of the architect G.E. Street (1824-1881), who was a productive High Victorian Gothic enthusiast. (Norman Shaw was Street's assistant from 1859 to 1863.) Webb became one of the founder members of the William Morris firm and was responsible for early furniture design, since Morris was interested in other things. Webb

*Three views of an exceptional roll-top desk by J.P. Seddon made of oak and inlaid with marquetry of various woods. Shown at the 1862 International Exhibition and rather owing something to Burges in the exuberance of the decoration (the drawer handles were ornamented with turquoise cameos, cabochon-cut malachite and ruby glass). By any standards a unique and expensive piece of furniture, like Shaw's bookcase, probably designed for his own use.*

*Photo: Courtesy Michael Whiteway and the Fine Art Society*

*A characteristic oak refectory table designed by Philip Webb for Morris and Co. Note the heavy 'revealed' construction and simplicity of line to which Webb, always a purist, adhered. The type was probably designed in the 1860s but was still advertised by the firm much later.*

*A Gothic cabinet of the Revival period, made by Gillows & Co. possibly to a design of Talbert's.*

designed Gothic, medieval-style oak tables, painted furniture and even leather panels and gesso decoration. He was responsible for a good deal of the William Morris & Co. furniture in the 1860s and onwards until others took over in the 1890s. Nonetheless his designs remained in the company's catalogues until much later.

### Bruce Talbert, 1838-1881

In 1867 Talbert published *Gothic Forms Applied to Furniture*. One of the objections to Victorian Gothic furniture is that it has a rather ecclesiastical flavour, redolent of vicarages and the headmaster's study — both perhaps uncomfortable images for a domestic interior. In a generation or so this imagery will doubtless have disappeared, but one of the advantages of Talbert's designs at the time was that they were less ecclesiastical and a bit more domesticated. His designs were influential and he had a grasp of construction as well as an understanding of decoration, although he was a bit fond of turned spindles and, again, had a tendency to enormously large scale. Pauline Agius has summarised the characteristics of the Talbertian or 'progressive', revolution of the 1870s as follows:

— straight lines, long strap hinges and ring handles
— the enrichment of mouldings with dentils and other archi-tecturally inspired ornaments
— tongue and groove planking sometimes set diagonally (Handley Read has pointed out that Seddon used this on the Morris cabinet of 1862, althouth this is not evident to anyone inspecting the piece externally in the Victoria and Albert Museum. Richard Charles and Eastlake also display it in their designs)
— cut through work and rows of spindles
— applied enamelled plates and painted panels
— inlay and occasional appropriate low relief carving in place of 'unmeaning scrolls'
— revealed construction showing dovetail and tenons (for some reason, Pugin and his followers thought this to be more 'honest' than concealed joints. Roll over, Chippendale!)
— the inset panel
— unstained oak merely oiled (sometimes resulting in a rather livid orange colour)

## Charles Lock Eastlake, 1836-1906

Published the book *Hints on Household Taste* of 1868, a down-to-earth sound-fellow approach with the influence of Webb, Burges and Talbert in his designs. Unlike the other reformers he was more in tune with domestic realities and his designs moderate the scale, which the others — including Talbert — were apt to use. It was as if, in Talbert's case, he were sometimes still working on the drawings of the Albert Memorial for Sir Giles Gilbert Scott. Eastlake, on the other hand, puts forward simple, honest construction, rational forms and less complex decoration, although he was capable of using the inlays, stained glass panels, bespindled galleries, diagonal tongued planking, inset panels, carved grooving and architectural mouldings that were features of the period — all on one piece!

Eastlake's book was very influential in England and America (where 'Eastlake' furniture was widely produced, not very accurately), yet he remains a designer, not a maker, and few pieces made exactly to his designs have been identified.

## William Burges

Architect famous for his decorative designs and furniture, mainly his French Gothic work of the 1860s, in which pieces of furniture aped little houses and castles. The sloping house-type roof with imitation tiles is a hallmark of Burges, who used the armoires of Northern France, with their iron

*(Above) 'Pet' sideboard by Talbert, made by Gillows in 1873 in oak, with carved creatures, foliage and a quotation in Latin across the back of an improving nature. (Arts and Crafts Movement designers became fond of doing the same quotational features on sideboards.)*

*(Right) A wardrobe in the Eastlake manner of the 1870s showing in simple measure the features characteristic of the genre: diagonal tongued-and-grooved planking to the doors, inlaid decoration, inset pillars, architectural mouldings and long strap hinges.*

bindings and painted decoration, as a model. His scholarship in Gothic was considerable but he was willing to use decoration of a classical, Renaissance or Japanese derivation on Gothic structures. He was well into Japanese ornament before the 1862 Exhibition and the flamboyant pieces painted with scenes from Chaucer or Malory reflect the medieval enthusiasms of this rich influential character who had a strong effect on the Morris firm in figurative techniques and on E.W. Godwin in terms of Anglo-Japanese taste. Burges furniture now fetches enormous sums of money.

## Richard Norman Shaw, 1831-1912

Celebrated architect, mostly domestic, but also of churches and public buildings. Started off using Gothic-ecclesiological styles, but soon moved to 'Old English' based on Kentish-Sussex Wealden houses of tile-hung and half-timbered types. In the 1870s, moved to 'Queen Anne' styles for mainly town houses and ended up using classical-baroque revival styles for public buildings. Subject of a superb biography by Andrew Saint (1976). The famous Gothic bookcase of 1860 in the Victoria and Albert Museum is of great stylistic interest but not typical (see below). His furniture designs included Queen Anne-style rush-seated corner chairs for Willesley, Cranbrook, Kent, stained green, in 1865; large plain Gothic-reformed settles, sideboards and beds à la Webb-Burges; and flimsier ebonised be-spindled chairs and furniture, Japanese and traditional in design. Little survives and no design can be dated after 1880. His designs are described as masculine and he liked corner chairs, which tends to reinforce that description. Knew Webb, Morris, Burges, Godwin, Voysey and many other famous architects, artists and designers. His pupils — Lethaby, Sydney Barnsley, Prior, Newton and Horsley jnr., became great forces in the Arts and Crafts Movement (q.v.) but Shaw, although encouraging them, did not belong nor did he admire that stylistic trend. Was united with Philip Webb in disliking the art nouveau work of the Century Guild and the Glasgow School (Mackintosh).

*Bookcase by Richard Norman Shaw now in the Victoria and Albert Museum. Shown in 1861 and again in the Medieval Court at the London International Exhibition of 1862. Produced at a time when Shaw was working for the great architect G.E. Street, and of a Gothic flamboyance not normally associated with Shaw. Made to Shaw's design by the carver James Forsyth to a standard of craftsmanship far higher than many of the Burges and Morris pieces but still an architectural structure, more allied to stone than wood, imitating a building rather than a piece of furniture. The style and embellishments are, however, fascinating, for the piece incorporates, within its oak structure, surfaces of rosewood, satinwood and bird's-eye maple. Much so-called 'honest' construction, with exposed dowels, joints and tenons; marquetry and ornamental motifs abound, with overlapping suns, flowers, peacock tails and part circles or 'pies' derived partly from guilloche carving on medieval church chests, partly from the whorls on Rossetti's picture frames. The piece was intended for Shaw's own use and is interesting in the early integration of Japanese motifs with Gothic forms. It has been suggested by Andrew Saint that the top gables were intended for the display of Shaw's few precious blue-and-white Nanking porcelain pots which he collected, again following Rossetti and Whistler and perhaps bought from his friend Arthur Liberty who was the first regular importer, or Murray Marks, another friend in that trade. It contained Shaw's pots, his books, secret possessions, correspondence and, underneath in the thin cupboard, his rolls of drawings. Not a piece of domestic furniture but a working architect's piece of self-indulgence. Shaw tired of the piece and gave it to his daughter's convent, where it was rediscovered in 1962.*

# Art Furniture — The Aesthetic Movement, 1865-1890

The term 'art furniture' tends nowadays to be superseded in auctioneers' jargon by 'Aesthetic Movement' or even 'art aesthetic' furniture so as to avoid confusion with art nouveau, or arts and crafts or, even, art deco. Art furniture was a term used in the late 1860s and on into the 1880s as a trendy name by firms considering themselves apart from ordinary manufacturers. It came, perhaps, as a result of the Aesthetic Movement, a term generally describing the middle class enthusiasm of the 1870s and 1880s for artistic matters, when art magazines, art pottery and art clothes were the 'in thing'.

The key piece which is always cited as highly influential in this type of furniture is a cabinet designed by T.E. Colcutt, made by a firm called Collinson & Lock, and exhibited at the London International Exhibition of 1871. It has many of the features of the black, ebonised furniture which became characteristic of the Art or Aesthetic Movement, namely painted and coved panels, bevelled-edged mirrors, rows of turned spindles and many straight lines in the design. Sometimes, instead of ebonising, dark woods such as black walnut were used or even wood stained green, as with William Morris whose green stain is said to have been discovered by Ford Madox Brown.

There is no doubt that this type of ebonised furniture, influenced by France, where the relevant cabinet makers were not called *ébénistes* for nothing, was very popular for about twenty years. Gillows and Shoolbred, reputable commercial firms, produced much ebonised furniture. Eventually, the fussily bracketed, bespindled, shelved and mirrored furniture fell out of fashion and the ebonised appearance, particularly when dusty (see Percy Wells' obsession with this, p.14) and secondhand is disliked by the modern antique trade so much that large quantities must have been broken up and lost forever.

*The celebrated cabinet designed by T.E. Colcutt, made by Collinson & Lock and exhibited at the International Exhibition of 1871. In ebonised wood with painted panels. This type of furniture was illustrated by Yapp (see* Pictorial Dictionary of British 19th Century Furniture Design) *and Shoolbred, Gillows and other manufacturers. It was much copied and must have been popular.*

*(Left) An Aesthetic Movement sideboard of good quality exhibiting many of the major characteristics of the type. Note that it is of ebonised wood with mahogany panels and incorporates a coved top à la Collcutt; a spindled ebonised gallery; bevelled panels and mirrors; many straight lines in the design.*
  *Photo: Courtesy Michael Whiteway*

*(Right) An ebonised Aesthetic Movement bureau bookcase, this time with painted panels of high quality depicting ladies in classical dress reclining on yet more ebonised spindled furniture. Again there is panelled construction and a cut-through gallery at the top.*

# Anglo-Japanese — E.W. Godwin and Art Furniture 1865-1890

The London International Exhibition of 1862 had on view the collection of Japanese artefacts of the first British consul, Sir Rutherford Alcock. It has been suggested by Pauline Agius that this collection had a strong influence on visitors but E.W. Godwin, who is associated inextricably with the style, was a friend of Burges (q.v.) who also had a large Japanese collection. Indeed the Gothic reformers were attracted to the ideals of Japanese society in the Pre-Raphaelite terms in which they conceived them. In addition to design characteristics, it was like the Gothic medieval society they admired — knights in armour bashing evil doers, artist-craftsmen treadling away, maidens sighing, a royalist structure with attendant priests, etc. etc. (It would be interesting now to get the reformers' reactions to the current return to our society of Japanese influence in its electro-mechanical, rather than medieval, form.)

Godwin is credited with the great originality of using Japanese answers to western furniture problems of design. He produced his celebrated sideboard (in the Victoria and Albert Museum) around 1867, showing how purely western pieces of furniture might benefit from Japanese concepts. Other versions of this sideboard and pieces of writing furniture were also produced by him in the 1860s and 1870s. Later, in 1877, a catalogue of Godwin's designs was produced by William Watt, a furniture producer, entitled *Art Furniture,* which was a sell-out, being reprinted in 1878. A lot of the furniture was ebonised and subsequent commercial producers of Anglo-Japanese or 'Art' furniture over the next fifteen years used ebonising

*A chair designed by E.W. Godwin for the Art Furniture Co. in 1867. Note the use of the stamped decoration on the leather-covered panel in the back — very similar to that on upholstered chair 248 in the Price Guide Section. The back spacing and uprights are somewhat 'Japanese' but the turned ringing in the uprights is similar to that used by Shaw and Morris contemporaneously and, later, by Arts and Crafts designers.*

*Celebrated sideboard designed by Godwin c.1867 now in the Victoria and Albert Museum. Made by the firm of Watt who published a catalogue entitled* Art Furniture *in 1877. The whole attraction of this design is its relationship and place as a milestone in the progression of designs towards the Modern Movement of the 20th century.*

27

as well as the painted and coved panels, bevelled-edged mirrors and rows of turned spindles characteristic of art furniture (q.v.).

A more detailed study is due on the influence of Japanese styles in British furniture. In his early days, around 1896, Charles Rennie Mackintosh (q.v.) hung up reproductions of Japanese prints in his basement room. It is said that the houses depicted in them would have had a strong effect on him, particularly in the relationship of space, line and form. Sir John Betjeman, in his letter published in David Joel's book of 1953 (see bibliography) and Joel himself made the point that the Anglo-Japanese craze at the end of the century gave a lot to Mackintosh, George Walton and their followers. Howarth, who first published in 1952, also pointed this out. It is not enough, therefore, simply to sniff at Japanese influences as a passing fad for a few fashion-conscious dandies. Burges, Godwin and Mackintosh are major figures in British furniture design of the period. The pity is that commercial copyists leapt on to the Godwin-inspired bandwagon and produced half-baked versions of 'Japanese' styles which eventually debased the whole art furniture movement. This is a pity because Godwin's original designs are quite delightful and now highly prized.

*Chair designed by Godwin c.1885 showing his design influences. The craze for Anglo-Japanese furniture became debased in the 1890s.*

*A tantalising piece of ebonised furniture — a secretaire bookcase showing the influence of both Burges and Godwin, both of them Japanese enthusiasts. Burges' influence is in the sloping, roofed top; the Japanese arrangement of the mirrors reflects(!) Godwin. Yet the three-panelled fall concealing the fitted writing interior and the rather square 'Chippendale' legs are derived from English origins. The sides are panelled in sloping tongued-and-grooved planking à la Eastlake; the open compartments like drawers between the legs may have been for rolls of small drawings or plans, for the piece is very architectural. It is almost as though Burges, Godwin, Eastlake and possibly Norman Shaw sat down together one rainy afternoon and designed a bureau for fun, then got James Forsyth to make it, for it is of a high quality cabinet work.*
*Photo: Courtesy Michael Whiteway*

# The Arts and Crafts Movement — Progressive Furniture (Art Nouveau)

C.R. Ashbee
M.H. Baillie Scott
Ernest and Sidney
   Barnsley
Ernest Gimson
Heal & Co.

William Lethaby
Liberty & Co.
Charles Rennie
   Mackintosh
A.H. Mackmurdo

William Morris & Co.
W.A.S. Benson
George Jack
Philip Webb
C.F.A. Voysey
George Walton

In the 1880s a number of architects and craftsmen formed guilds and associations in an attempt to get away from the prevailing mass-produced debased styles or reproductions of the commercial furniture trade. They were inspired by William Morris and Ruskin. These guilds and societies sprang up in various parts of the country, Mackmurdo having founded the Century Guild in 1882. The Arts and Crafts Exhibition Society held its first exhibition in 1888 (with very little furniture) and followed this up in 1889, 1890, 1893, 1896 and 1899. Some of the progressive designers, like Mackintosh and Voysey, merit separate treatment as independent spirits, but from many followers of the movement there was a far too slavish adherence to the hatred of all machinery and to the condemnation of the whole commercial furniture world as being run by tasteless tradesmen, which was ridiculous. In some cases this culminated in a withdrawal to rustic workshops in such places as the Cotswolds to live and work out an idealised life which ignored the age of machinery.

It is perhaps too easy to deride the Cotswold and other rural handicraft makers as ostriches now. It was not so much their preoccupation with the avoidance of machines that we should remember. For Gimson and his followers were not the equivalent of the modern back-to-craftwork brigade, retiring to subsistence living in the country, throwing pots, weaving ponchos and rushing seats in competition with India, Korea or Taiwan. They were unique designers and craftsmen who wished to be different. Gimson made pieces that are not always successful and pieces which are clearly 18th century-inspired but they are individual and his example was beneficial to many people. Certainly none of the Cotswold craftsmen were prolific; the comparative rarity of pieces by Gimson and the Barnsleys has perhaps established a high value for them, although it is hard to say yet what kind of market exists for their work outside museums.

*Chairs by A.H. Mackmurdo, founder of the Century Guild in 1882. The tall chair below is said to have influenced many later designers, while the sinuous forms in the back of the chair above were said to be influential on the art nouveau movement.*

The ironic thing is that while those who followed Morris were evolving their curious attitudes towards production methods, the firm of William Morris & Co. was turning out the sort of furniture which met the contemporary demands of the trade, as the catalogues show. It was, of course, perfectly possible to turn out commercial furniture that was both well-designed and well-constructed, which is why Heal & Co., in addition to Morris, are usually included in the category of progressive producers. Liberty is more often associated with art nouveau furniture, with 'quaint' associations.

The various names lumped together in this broad category cover a variety of architects and designer-craftsmen who form a loosely-related group in terms of ideals or personal relationships. There are many inconsistencies, and the movement's relationship with art nouveau is liable to confuse the layman. It is odd that Mackmurdo is often associated with the origination of art nouveau designs, because the Arts and Crafts Exhibition Society considered art nouveau to be degenerate, a sinuous, plastic Continental form that had no place in their scheme of things. What is more, Mackmurdo's designs are mainly quite severe and only one chair gives rise to his association with art nouveau. Voysey's designs were influential on Continental art nouveau but he disliked the foreign version intensely.

Mackintosh exhibited with the Arts and Crafts Exhibition Society twice, in 1896 and 1899, but his designs were disapproved of as being too art nouveau in manner. There are, clearly, many similarities between the British and the probably precedent Continental forms but in essence the main difference is that the British is more rectilinear and less plastic than the Continental. The reader is recommended to look at the comparison in *British Furniture 1880-1915* by Pauline Agius (pp.92-3) to get a visual impression of the major differences.

### A.H. Mackmurdo, 1851-1942
Founder of the Century Guild in 1882 and virulently opposed to the prevailing commercial productions. Credited with the 'tall chair' movement's origination by virtue of his chair exhibited in 1886 (see illustration on page 29, bottom left) which was not well received by contemporary critics. It was, however, a very clean and simple design when compared with the turned spindled galleries of commercial art furniture and he was very influential in textiles and wallpapers on European art nouveau. His furniture designs are not, however, particularly consistent with each other and reflect a variety of approaches. The sinuous design in the back of his other, famous, chair (see illustration on page 29, top left) is partly derived from Blake, partly from the Pre-Raphaelites and partly from plant designs such as the tulip. The fretwork is ornamental, not part of the structure which is severe in style.

*A cabinet with floral inlay designed by George Jack, who took over at William Morris & Co. from Philip Webb. Jack was a very decorative carver and inlayer and many of his pieces are much more sophisticated than one associates with the Arts and Crafts Movement c.1895.*

*Bureau by the architect C.F.A. Voysey c.1896. Voysey designed very restful rooms in which plain oak furniture of original lines contributed to the lightness of design. Now thought of as art nouveau in manner but in fact nothing like the Continental version.*

*Table by George Walton*

*Chair by Charles Rennie Mackintosh.*

### William Morris & Co.

Morris himself was not particularly interested in furniture but he and his associates, George Jack, William Lethaby, Philip Webb and W.A.S. Benson, all sent work to the Arts and Crafts Society's Exhibitions. George Jack designed furniture for Morris & Co. for many years and is associated with marquetry inlays and carving, on which he published a book. Webb and Benson designed for Morris before Jack, with Webb being the most influential. The output of Morris & Co. seems to have been either inexpensive, good commercial stuff like the Sussex rush-seated chairs and general furniture; or very, very expensive elaborate cabinets, etc. The point about Morris's difficulties with handicrafts has been well made by Charlotte Gere: because he was committed to hand weaving his 'Hammersmith' carpets, their cost dictated a selling price at the end of the 19th century of £4 a square yard — a modern equivalent would be at least £100 a square yard.

### William Lethaby, 1857-1931

Included because of his associations with Morris and Gimson (qq.v.). One of the founders of Kenton & Co. (see Gimson) and not primarily a furniture designer, but was Principal of the Central School of Arts and Crafts.

### C.R. Ashbee, 1863-1942

Founder of another Guild, in 1888. Worked in the East End, teaching young people. Liked the idea of several craftsmen combining their skills on one piece. Little of his furniture has been identified.

### C.F.A. Voysey, 1857-1941

An important figure. Rather an austere purist in character but very influential in domestic architectural design. Often designed houses complete with furnishings and made a good living from textile pattern design as well. Nearly always used oak in plain surfaces but with complex hinge or metalwork decoration in a style now generally thought of as art nouveau (which he hated).

### M.H. Baillie Scott, 1865-1945

Another architect, now famous for the 'Manxman' piano design. Lived in Bedford and was associated, in 1902, with the publication of *A Book of Furniture* by the firm J.P. White, a high class joinery producer.

### George Walton, 1867-1933

Another architect, from Glasgow, who was, like Mackintosh, commissioned to do work for Miss Cranston's Tea Rooms. Designed quite a lot of furniture as well as other work.

### Charles Rennie Mackintosh, 1868-1923

Now almost notorious in antique trade circles following the sale of one of his cabinets for £90,000 to the Glasgow authorities who, between them, have the largest collection of his work. Generally acknowledged to be brilliant as a designer of furniture that falls into the category of Fine Art rather than furniture. Mackintosh was a designer who was, if anything, inhibited by the use of wood as a material and did not follow those principles of construction and craftsmanship which the Gothic reformers and most progressives would have insisted upon. In this sense his designs sometimes are mildly 'wrong' when seen out of the context for which they were designed despite their brilliance and originality. Some were even badly made and some chairs could fall apart if sat upon for long.

His furniture is often decorated with motifs such as the weeping rose or shapes which puzzle the viewer. Handley-Read has made the point that "there is also the evidence among his decorations of a curious neuroticism — the 'spook school' element evoked by weeping spirits, disconcerting eyes and tall figures caged among roses" — a marvellously accurate description.

Mackintosh has merited many studies and there are excellent books

available about him. In some ways he has been almost too much written up. Yet he is a major figure, of European influence, and there is no doubt his pieces will be coveted by museums. See illustrations.

**Ernest and Sidney Barnsley, 1863-1926 and 1865-1926**
Both were founders, with Gimson, of Kenton & Co. Ernest made furniture for himself, but Sidney, with whom he moved to the Cotswolds — with Gimson — in 1895, was an archetypal artist-craftsman and worked at his bench until 1924. Sidney made robust, bow-fronted planked pieces which were dubbed the 'butter tub and carpenter's bench style'.

*A cabinet by Mackintosh shown closed and open. Furniture by Mackintosh is now a rich man's possession, due to the fervour of the Glasgow authorities and other museums (the Louvre was the underbidder for the £90,000 cabinet) to purchase his work. For an appreciation of Mackintosh's furniture, a read of the book* Charles Rennie Mackintosh, The Complete Furniture etc., *by Roger Billcliffe is essential.*

*Pieces by the Barnsleys showing a walnut desk by Ernest Barnsley with characteristic inlay and in a style much associated now with Gimson and Gordon Russell and a dresser by Sidney Barnsley, again somewhat after Gimson but with modifications. Exhibited in 1903 and not admired by the critic of the* Cabinet Maker.

*Cabinet by Ernest Gimson and table designed by him c.1908 but actually a version executed in the 1930s by his successor, Peter Waals. Gimson was quite fond of tightly-drawered cabinets of renaissance inspiration as well as his more celebrated fielded oak panelling on more bucolic pieces.*
*Cabinet courtesy Michael Whiteway*
*Table courtesy Sotheby's Belgravia*

## Ernest Gimson, 1864-1919

Doyen of the Cotswold craftsmen and capable of superb designs. One of the founders of a firm called Kenton & Co. in 1890, with the Barnsleys, Lethaby, etc. It folded in 1892, and he subsequently moved to Gloucestershire. He was not so much a craftsman himself, like Barnsley, but was very familiar with all the processes, having worked with J.D. Sedding next door to Morris & Co. By 1903 he was established at Sapperton, where his Daneway workshops turned out the pieces with distinctive fielded panels and through joints in the 'revealed construction' manner beloved of the reformers. This is not entirely representative, however; some of his work is very light and elegant, and he inspired many followers.

*Oak sideboard by Ernest Gimson shown at the 1900 Paris Exhibition. A characteristic fielded-panel design also influential on other modern designers.*

*Cupboard chest in holly green with chamfers picked out in bright red, by Ambrose Heal 1899.*

### Heal & Co.

Inspired by Ambrose Heal, Jnr., who was not trained as an architect, but as a craftsman, the well-known Tottenham Court Road firm showed how good design could be allied to commercial production. Pieces from 1895 onwards are now somewhat sought after and merit attention, particularly if involved in any of the well-received exhibitions that the firm staged.

### Liberty & Co.

Very much associated with high quality art nouveau furniture. Had earlier imported Moorish styles, but the art nouveau furniture was often designed by George Walton.

### Postscript

It is interesting to note that in Germany the work of Gimson inspired a movement of architects and craftsmen to set up the Werkbund in 1907. The Germans were less worried about the use of machinery than the socialist-inspired followers of Morris, who were so obsessed with the social and craftsmanship effects of the industrial revolution. In 1914, inspired by the Deutsche Werkbund, a group in Britain formed the Design and Industries Association to bring the artist and the manufacturer together. Ambrose Heal, William Lethaby and others were involved from the start. Exhibitions were held in the 1930s and the association was still influential on Joel when he wrote in 1953.

*Wardrobe by Ambrose Heal c.1900. Characteristic Arts and Crafts Movement design, this, mainly oak inlaid with box and holly in chequered patterns.*

*Plate rack and dresser by Ambrose Heal c.1906. Designed for production in quantity and of good clean lines which influenced Wells (q.v.) and others later.*

# The Nineteen Twenties, 1918-1930

| | | |
|---|---|---|
| Maurice Adams | Romney Green | Gordon Russell |
| Art Deco | Ambrose Heal | Peter Waals |
| Frank Brangwyn | The Joels | Percy Wells |
| | Liberty & Co. | |

*A classic example of cinematic 'Jaco-bethan' oak furniture, c.1930. The bureau is on an unnecessarily bulbous-legged stand — the bulbs are there merely to state the 'style' and the drawers are embellished with machine-carved curvilinear deco-ration. Made in a cheap oak and stained dark brown to give an aged effect.*

It is perhaps unfair to lump everything that happened in the 1920s under one heading, but we are as yet at an early stage for real assessment. In market and price terms the period is still subject to fluctuations of fashion. Basically, the split between trade reproductions and the gradually emerging Modern Movement continued but the First World War had changed society and attitudes so much that there was, in Britain, a rather quiet period with little development and progress in original design. Gimson died in 1919; Voysey and Mackintosh found themselves completely out of fashion. Art nouveau was dead. There were, however, others who carried on and made progress.

In 1925 the Salon des Art Décoratifs was held in Paris, which has now given the name 'art deco' to the styles associated with it. Joel has claimed that the 1925 Paris Exhibition had few repercussions in Britain. The French furniture exhibited had little or no British influence apart from an acknowledgement of Morris's principles. If we take art deco in the sense that it is loosely used now, there are many indications of the style well before 1925, much as there were of Chippendale designs before 1755. A use of some of the motifs and asymmetrical zig-zags was already transferring from the use of abstract art in textiles and carpets to furniture, but it was not until the 1930s that the heyday of asymmetrical design seems to have impressed its spiky edges on furniture design.

## Trade Production (or Reproduction)
1. **'Jacobethan'.** The 1920s saw the mass-production of possibly the cheapest and nastiest versions of 'Jacobean' furniture made up to that time. Joel has pointed out that the use of the cheapest American oak, covered in a

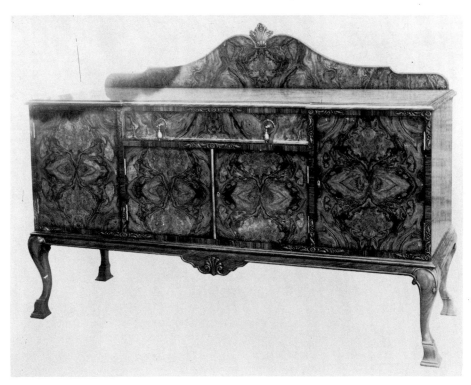

*The amazing 'burr walnut be-dappled'. A sideboard of c.1930 in multi-quartered walnut veneer, giving the effect of a series of Rorschach ink blot tests. A really popular style in the 1930s.*

*An oak pedestal in the 'Jacobethan' style so popular during this period.*

sticky black jollop, enabled mass-producers to turn out really detestable furniture. The bulbous legs which appear to have been universally adopted as a mark of the breed were modified to less circular and more cinematic art deco forms but without alleviating the unpleasantness of the species.

Not all oak reproduction furniture was mass-produced in this fashion, of course. There are some quite reasonably proportioned oak dining tables and dressers from the period — Maurice Adams illustrates one or two better examples. What is ironic is that it was probably the Morris-inspired reformed furniture which gave rise to a widespread taste for medieval-style oak furniture. This taste was to be satisfied by the so-called Jacobean dining suites of the 1920s to the present day. Poor Morris!

**2. Burr Walnut Bedappled.** It is hard to fix exactly the starting point of the burr walnut furniture of initially Queen Anne design origin that became so popular in the late 1920s and continued into the 1930s. Maurice Adams, who considered himself an original designer, in his book of 1926 shows dressing tables and other items which are of pure Queen Anne origin but modernised and adapted for present day needs. These are available in highly-figured walnut and in the burr form, principally as bedroom furniture items and dining furniture such as sideboards.

The use of richly-burred walnut in semi-reproduction furniture of this type could well pre-date 1914, however. It would be quite logical to suppose that the reproduction trade could move to the production of sideboards such as those illustrated, gradually modified to a more 'modern' style. What is certain is that by the end of the 1920s and in the 1930s the use of burr walnut had evolved a distinctive genre of furniture all of its own, generally associated with bedrooms. Old antique trade craftsmen still tell stories of the burr walnut oval 'loo' table tops which they split down the centre to form two half-oval bedheads in the 1920s and 1930s, when Victorian furniture was out of fashion (the bases belonging to the tops kept the workshops warm, chopped into the stove). The cabriole leg was back with a vengeance and stayed in rooms of 'good taste' for thirty years or more.

*More burr walnut bedappled, this time for its more familiar setting of the bedroom, in a dressing chest and table. The burr variety can be more confusing to the eye than this matched-figure type (see Wardrobe section) but this is quite spectacular enough. Note the stubby cabrioles which complete the 'Queen Anne' association, necessary for 1930s 'good taste'.*

36

*A bedside cabinet by Gordon Russell of 1929. Note, once again, the stretchered legs and the ebony and holly stringing. The use of wooden handles of a semi-streamlined design similar to that on the door is also a Gordon Russell characteristic.*

**3. Plain Furniture.** Perhaps inspired by Percy 'Dusty' Wells, there was a considerable amount of oak and hardwood furniture made in a style one can only refer to as 'Plain'. *The Woodworker* magazine of the 1920s is a rich source of such designs. Alleviated slightly by the addition of machine-made mouldings or beadings, it is a kind of cross between an attenuated Jacobean and 'gramophone cabinet style' — square, utilitarian and rather depressing. Plywood was creeping in. Made for the thousands of semi-detached and other small houses being built at the time, it was doubtless cheap and functional but of little durability.

### Peter Waals
Waals was the foreman at Gimson's workshops and, after Gimson's death, carried on his tradition until his own death. He was trained in Holland, but his pieces continue the Gimson tradition of fielded panels, boxwood and ebony inlaid broad stringing lines, using solid English-grown oak and walnut. He was more than just a foreman, being a gifted craftsman and designer.

### Gordon Russell, 1892-1980
Actually started before this period. Initially a follower of Gimson and based at Broadway, Worcester, but by no means a Luddite and showed how machinery could be used to turn out fine individual furniture. Considered now to be sufficiently important to be in the Victoria and Albert Museum. Used oak and walnut of English origin, usually in the solid. His brother, Professor Richard Russell, was Professor of Woodwork at the Royal College of Art and they worked together. The use of the stretchered pedestal design was applied to desks, dressing tables and sideboards and is distinctive.

*A 1924 sideboard by Gordon Russell, straight down in line from Gimson's designs. The stretchered square legs were used uniformly on desks, sideboards, dressers, dressing tables and other furniture. The piece is made in solid English walnut.*

*A wardrobe by Peter Waals, foreman at Gimson's workshops (Gimson didn't make furniture himself), who carried on after Gimson's death. Clearly in the continuing Gimson tradition, using solid walnut with fielded panelling and ebony and holly banding or stringing. The piece even reiterates the ogee foot used so badly by Gimson on a square-section chair leg design.*

### Romney Green, 1872-1945

Belongs partly to the earlier pre-1914 period, because he exhibited at the Arts and Crafts Society Exhibition in 1906. He had a workshop at Strand-on-the-Green, Chiswick, where he worked in the 1920s and 1930s. According to Joel he was a Wrangler, a poet, writer and teacher who gave up teaching to follow the Morris tradition of earning a living with one's hands. It would be interesting to know how many educated intellectuals were inspired by this ideal in the 1920s and 1930s. At one stage Evelyn Waugh was apprenticed to a cabinet maker or carpenter with such an idea in mind (having failed at Oxford). Fortunately for literature, Waugh's natural character overcame this project.

### Percy Wells

Percy Wells was Head of the Cabinet Department at the Shoreditch Technical Institute, deep in the heart of London's furniture manufacturing industry. Reference has already been made in detail to his books and attitudes — see pages 14-15. Wells' own furniture is highly practical and simple in line but he perhaps over-imbibed Morris's brand of idealistic socialism or else was over-inspired by the Garden City concept of a Fabian nature. Obsessed about dust-catching surfaces.

### Maurice Adams

Published *My Book of Furniture* in 1926. By no means a recluse of the Cotswold type. His book gives the impression of considerable self-promotion and of a realistic commercial attitude to production and marketing.

*Chair by Romney Green.*

*A sideboard designed by Percy 'Dusty' Wells, c.1925. Characteristic of Wells' very simple forms which go back to Heal (q.v.).*

*Dressing table by Maurice Adams, 1926.*

### Heal & Son Ltd.
Continued to produce furniture of restrained, clean modern design of a kind in the best tradition.

### Liberty & Co.
Another firm which, like Heal, drew commendation from contemporary designers for the quality and design of its furniture. Associated earlier with many art nouveau designers and with 'quaint' variations.

### Frank Brangwyn, 1867-1956
Better known as a painter and designer, but in fact started designing furniture from 1900. His furniture tends to be in solid English woods such as oak, walnut, and even cherry.

*A chair by Frank Brangwyn bought at Bonhams for £1,200 in 1979. Made in solid walnut to Brangwyn's design by the firm of E. Pollard & Co.*

*A pedestal writing table in veneered Australian walnut with ebonised bands and Ivorine handles from Liberty & Co.*

*Oak desk designed by Ambrose Heal, 1929. The shape of the furniture, and the contrasting surfaces, achieved by a parquetry approach to the deep drawer fronts, are typical of what is now loosely called 'art deco' furniture.*

*A dressing table designed by J.F. Johnson for Heal & Son Ltd. in 1926. Made in Indian laurel and ebony. The piece shows quite modern mass-production styling and execution while retaining quality, but the tapering curved legs must be subject to fashionable vagaries in popularity.*

## Betty Joel Ltd.

Included here mainly because of David Joel's book of 1953 in which Morris and Gimson are perhaps over-praised. It is a refreshing work in many ways despite the author's prejudices. His invitation to John Betjeman, Paul Reilly and Richard Russell to differ with him in print in his own book shows how open-minded he must have been. The firm started up in 1921 but really belongs to a volume covering a later period than this work.

*Illustrations by David Joel of oak 'horrors' of the 1930 era, now sold partly as Jacobethan, partly as art deco.*

*Six typical pieces of furniture from the* Studio Yearbook of Decorative Art, *1930. The sideboard (top left) and the table (bottom left) are designed by Francis Dagley and both owe a great deal to the Ernest Gimson-Peter Waals school of furniture. With the exception of the wardrobe (bottom right) the other pieces are by Edward Barnsley, who has carried on the tradition of Ernest and Sidney Barnsley from his workshops in Hampshire.*

# Price Guide Section

We now move on to the price guide section of the book. The same format as *The Price Guide to Antique Furniture* has been adopted, that of grouping together pieces of similar types and discussing variations in quality and value.

Where the Antique Collectors' Club price guide format differs from others which have followed it, is that the background to the pieces themselves is discussed and they can be seen in the ranges of quality available. Thus it is hoped that the reader will acquire a knowledge of the huge variety of furniture that appeared during this period.

# BUREAU BOOKCASES

Bureau bookcases appear to have languished a bit in the mid-Victorian period. There was a continuation of production of the sub-classical types of the 1840s but on the whole writing was at desks and books were in cabinets. Perhaps the pieces of Burges and Shaw exhibited in 1862 revived a taste for bureau bookcases; anyway by the 1880s they were back in swing and by the 1890s the Edwardian Sheraton bureau bookcase in mahogany was being reproduced in huge numbers.

1 (right) An ebonised Aesthetic Movement bureau bookcase with a fretted top, painted panels, panelled construction and turned supports typical of the Art Furniture Movement.

*c.1880*
*£450 — £700*

2 The rather tantalising piece possibly by Godwin-Burges-Eastlake-Shaw discussed in the Furniture Styles Data on the Anglo-Japanese period (p. 28). Here it is shown with the fall open to reveal the carefully-fitted interior.

*c.1880*          *Price at auction in 1978 £1,250*

3 An oak bureau bookcase of a type illustrated by several furniture makers in the 1900-1910 period. Similar designs occur in Graham & Banks c.1899 in mahogany, J.S. Henry 1900, Timms and Webb 1904 and Norman & Stacey's catalogue of c.1910, showing how commercial manufacturers followed the progressive furniture movement. The copper hinges to the bookcase doors, with their distinctive shaping, are 'art nouveau' in inspiration, but the piece is too rectilinear for Continental origins. The fretting of the bookshelves and the leaded glass doors are typical of the period, as is the rather quirky arrangement of drawers and enormous pigeon holes. The lantern has been added later by a rather unsympathetic soul, doubtless anxious to penetrate the central gloom inherent in the design.

*1900-1910*          *£150 — £250*

5 (right) A mahogany bureau bookcase which aims at being a reproduction of a late 18th century piece. Once again, however, the Edwardian desire to go slightly one better than the original has given the game away. The falls of 18th century mahogany bureaux were not quarter veneered in the way this one has been, giving a diamond-shaped effect to the figure. Nor was the inlaid boxwood stringing arranged in an elaborately curved patterned panel. The glazing bar arrangement on the bookcase doors could also probably be shown to be a later form.

*1900-1920*        *£300 — £500*

4 A mahogany bureau bookcase of George III 'design', with a broken pediment above the bookcase and satinwood banding throughout. A good three foot wide reproduction which, apart from its missing or broken front bracket feet, follows the original line quite correctly. The Midland Furnishing Company sold an almost identical version for £6. 6. 0. in 1910. Note that the bracket feet are damaged at the front. These bureaux are now standard 'trade' items and many of them still exist. The value of this example is helped by the curved broken pediment.

*1900-1925*        *£550 — £750*

6 A Sheraton style bureau-cabinet on square tapering legs ending in block feet. The upper cabinet is fitted with bevelled plate glass doors. There is a hinged, folding top to the writing area, which folds over to give a greater surface area and is lined with leather. The roller shutter slides back to reveal pigeon holes and drawers inside.

*1900-1910*        *£500 — £750*

7 (right) A 3ft. wide mahogany bureau bookcase on thin cabriole legs, of a type much produced from Edwardian times into the 1930s. The top, glazed cabinet has a reasonably robust approach to life but the legs are well and truly mean in proportion. It may be useful, it may be neatly made but the mass-produced look is deeply ingrained upon it.

*1900-1930*                                                          *£250 — £400*

8 (left) A chinoiserie lacquered double-domed bureau book-case in the Queen Anne style on bun feet. In this case the makers have decided on a bureau form incorporating a knee-hole, which is not a version very often found in the original period of 1710-1730 to which the style relates, but it is possible. The gilded carving on top of the domes incorporates scroll and leaf forms. The bun feet are to give it an 'early' look, i.e. to imply that the piece belongs to the transition from William-and-Mary bun feet (1690-1710) to Queen Anne but before bracket feet came into greater fashion (1710 onwards). Obviously requiring enormous time and skill to produce but lesser quality versions (without the top carving) are still made by the trade, often in a green colour, and sold to the U.S.A. for about £2,000 F.O.B. for subsequent auctioneering as 'period' and massively increased margin. This high-quality piece was made around 1920 and is pretty faithful to the original proportion and feel of the period except for the slightly thin top mouldings — although the makers would claim that this thinness is justified when top carving and gilding is involved, since the eye does not rest on the top moulding but goes up immediately to the gilded tops.

*c.1920*                                                          *£2,000 — £4,000*

9 (left) A characteristic oak 'Jacobethan' bureau bookcase on stretchered bulbous feet. The leaded glazing bars are typical and the geometric mouldings to the fall and drawer fronts — to give that 'Jacobean' look — are to be found on most versions.

*1925-1935*                                    *£200 — £350*

## BUREAU BOOKCASES — Elongated Edwardian

> The Elongated Edwardian bureaux described later were often available in a bureau bookcase form, although the bookcase above was often smaller than that of 18th century types. Leaded lights and quaint shapes were often used.

10 An oak bureau bookcase with fall open to show the pigeon holes inside. There is a centre cupboard above the fall, with circular leaded-light door. Above this, the top shelf sports a weirdly-carved pediment and finials. The whole piece is a gesture towards the Progressive and art nouveau influences of the period. Small — 2ft.6ins. wide and 5ft.3ins. high — so really quite a desirable size for modern rooms.

*1900-1915*                    *£100 — £180*

11 An oak bureau bookcase which is only a brief development further from the previous bureau. Note the side bookshelves, also a feature of No. 3. The upper shelves are useful but the huge gap below the fall could surely have been used better. The fall is carved with scrollwork and the odd, quirky pierced decoration is, presumably Progressive.

*1900-1915*                    *£90 — £150*

12 (left) A more coherent oak bureau bookcase design with the flat capped top rail of the Edwardian period which stemmed from Voysey and the original Progressive designers. The centre cupboard above the open fall again has a leaded-light door but is rectangular in sympathy with the rest of the piece, including the panelled cupboard doors below the fall. The only place where over-exuberance may have set in is in the rather Islamic arching of the alcoves containing the vases.

*1900-1915*                    *£100 — £180*

13 An oak bureau bookcase with a conventional lower half but fitted with leaded-light doors to the upper glazed cupboard, incorporating stained glass, which adds to value.

*1900-1915*                    *£120 — £200*

15 (above) A more conventional version of the previous oak bureau bookcase without leading in the glass doors of the upper half. Back in 1910 or so the difference in price between this and the previous one was ten shillings — five bob for leading each glass door.

*1900-1910*                    *£100 — £180*

16 (right) An oak bureau bookcase which owes something to the dresser in its design which is simple and pleasing. These pieces, of characteristically small proportions — 5ft.9ins. high and 2ft.9ins. wide — will be enthusiastically collected for their use in small rooms one day.

*1900-1920*                    *£100 — £160*

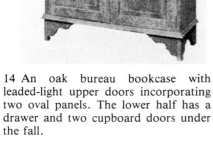

14 An oak bureau bookcase with leaded-light upper doors incorporating two oval panels. The lower half has a drawer and two cupboard doors under the fall.

*1900-1920*                    *£150 — £220*

## BUREAUX — bonheurs-du-jour

The bonheur-du-jour of French Empire inspiration appears to have died out in its early 19th century form, but during the Victorian 'Louis XIV' rococo period it re-emerged in burr or figured walnut as an elegant French piece. The examples show how the type prevailed through the vagaries of fashion as a suitable desk for a lady of means.

17 A walnut bonheur-du-jour of very French inspiration but in fact made by an English reproducer, with locks by a Birmingham firm. The boxwood inlays are of stylised flowers and semi-naturalistic forms. The two upper cupboards flanking the central mirror have glazed doors and pierced brass gallery rails above. The fitted interior has a well. An interesting example of how the Louis XV-rococo style, popular in England in its own adapted form, could be more faithfully reproduced — with variations, of course — almost as the local English form was dying. C. & R. Light illustrate a very similar model in their 1881 catalogue.

*1860-1885*       *£950 — £1,100*

18 (above) A satinwood inlaid bonheur-du-jour with a central domed mirror flanked by cupboard doors inlaid with marquetry. The square tapering legs curve elegantly outwards towards the ends. Altogether a very delicate and finely-made piece of Edwardian lady's equipment.

*1900-1910*       *£900 — £1,400*

19 (left) A mahogany bonheur-du-jour in the Sheraton manner on tapering square section legs ending in castors. The inlaid decoration is of flowers, patera and husks. The front surface folds over outwards to provide an extra area of writing surface, supported by pulling out the drawer, which has a baize-lined top edge to prevent scratching.

*1900-1910*       *£700 — £950*

20 A quite elegant writing table or bonheur-du-jour in the Edwardian Sheraton manner, with extensive inlays in boxwood and ivory. The drawers are banded in satinwood. The tapering square section legs end in brass castors and are connected by curving cross stretchers. The arcaded central section of the top is mirrored behind and the spindled top gallery sports characteristic finials.

*1895-1910*       *£800 — £1,200*

# BUREAUX — cylinder front

The cylinder front became a popular Edwardian form usually associated with higher quality bureaux. It was, of course, due to the popularity in revival of late 18th/early 19th century furniture of the Sheraton type that this vogue took place. Cylinder fronts still tend to be highly regarded despite the fact that they are somewhat subject to damage due to splitting and warpage in centrally heated conditions. Warpage can cause them to jam or lock in one position and repairs can be expensive.

21 A rosewood cylinder bureau, inlaid with marquetry dolphins, flowers and stringing lines. The arched cresting rail has an applied reeded or gadrooned vase and is a feature of much Edwardian furniture (without the vase). The square tapering legs end in castors. Inside the tambour top there is a pull-out writing surface and a fitted interior.

*1900-1910*                    *£700 — £900*

22 (above) A rather plain mahogany cylinder front bureau with three long drawers and mounted on bracket feet. The drawers and cylinder fall are crossbanded in satinwood in the characteristic Sheraton manner.

*1900-1910*                    *£350 — £500*

23 (left) A mahogany cylinder fall bureau in a somewhat Chippendale style of execution with Chinese fretted brackets at the tops of the square tapering legs. Note the carved decoration, which includes lion-mask handles to the cylinder fall.

*c.1920*                    *£450 — £600*

## BUREAUX — Elongated Edwardian

Following the popularity of the Progressive designers and the influence of Voysey and others, there was a move by the trade, around 1900, to produce designs in the required manner. This resulted in an entirely unique species of elongated bureaux, slightly, but ever so slightly, art nouveau in manner, using a much thinner depth of section, few drawers, if any, and often with elongated hinges to the fall in an 'artistic' design. The following section shows a selection of the bureaux; the bureau bookcases have a separate section to themselves.

24 (right) A typical example of the elongated species with stamped bronze handle and elongated hinges to the fall. Note that there are no drawers — only bookshelves below and a typical bookshelf round the top, formed by a solid wooden cresting rail.

*c.1900-1910*                    *£50 — £100*

25 An oak fall-front elongated bureau of the three foot wide, but much less deep, version preferred by the early 20th century. These slenderer — or should it be narrower — versions of the old 18th century invention, seem to have met a need for bureaux for smaller rooms. This is a very straightforward version with a simple interior and three drawers under.

*1900-1920*                    *£50 — £100*

26 A roll-top version of these oak bureaux with shelf above, pigeon holes inside but no drawer under — just shelves. Roll top adds to price.

*1900-1920*                    *£80 — £120*

27 (left) A fall-front oak bureau with a pierced fretted gallery round the top (also of oak) and with a drawer and two shelves under the fall. This generic type has been utterly despised until lately, when the use of the piece, the way it occupies little space, and the fact that it has been cheap, have suddenly made it a regular feature of many 'antique' shops.

*1900-1920*              *£50 — £100*

28 (right) A small oak roll-top bureau with a wooden top gallery rail intended as a bookshelf. The inside is neatly fitted with pigeon holes and there is a drawer and shelves under.

*1900-1920*              *£80 — £120*

29 An oak bureau which has a variation from the previous examples in the classic Edwardian shaping of the top rail. That central semi-circular arch is a very popular feature of the period (see Sideboards for similar examples). It may be thought that since these bureaux have only recently become a feature of the stock of 'antique' shops, there will have been little incentive to fake them or gerrymander about with them as yet. Not so: the author was recently offered one which turned out to have been re-fitted inside, repaired, improved and generally cobbled together from bits. So be warned.

*1900-1915*              *£50 — £100*

30 An oak fall-front bureau with a pierced top shelf which exhibits a heart shape and two art nouveau-ish leaves. Otherwise nothing remarkable.

*1900-1915*              *£50 — £100*

31 A small oak bureau (2ft.2ins. wide) of the same genre but with a dash of art nouveau shaping to the top shelf. Pigeon holes inside and shelves under, as before.

*1900-1915*              *£40 — £80*

32 (left) An oak bureau on stand with curved legs and shelf stretcher. The drawer under the fall, and the fall itself, are inlaid with the boxwood and ebony chequered banding ever popular in Arts and Crafts design. The top shelf is pierced to show a motif of indeterminate sort.

*1900-1915*                    *£50 — £100*

33 (right) An oak bureau on stand with bobbinised front legs to give an 'old oak' effect, relevant to the moulding on the fall, slightly 'Jacobean' in character. The ring handles are a Sheraton design.

*1900-1920*                    *£50 — £100*

## BUREAUX — reproduction, on bracket feet

The bureau seems to have languished (except as a bonheur-du-jour) until nearly the end of the 19th century when it enjoyed a revival in various forms but particularly in reproduction Sheraton style. The illustrations in this section trace the main types of bracket foot bureaux up to 1930. We have included those with solid plinths in this section also, since all the others are raised on legs of differing types.

34 A mahogany bureau of 18th century design, fairly faithfully reproduced. With three long drawers and a fitted interior. A fairly wide bureau — 3ft.6ins. — on bracket feet, which is so simple in following the 18th century original without unnecessary decoration that one feels it might easily pass off as an 18th century piece.

*1900-1930*                    *£350 — £500*

35 A mahogany bureau of late 18th century 'design', inlaid with stringing lines in boxwood and with marquetry panels, in the centre of which is a chinoiserie scene. Such inlaid panels require considerable expertise to produce and it is a high quality piece but, like so many Edwardian inlaid items, the decoration is just that little bit too flowery for comfort.

*1900-1910*                    *£600 — £900*

36 (left) A typical, almost classic, Edwardian Sheraton bureau, 2ft.6ins. wide, made in mahogany with satinwood crossbanding. There is a shell inlay in the centre of the fall, which is almost regulation, not to say *de rigueur*. Hundreds of these once-despised bureaux are now being sold by antique shippers to all parts of the globe.

*1900-1910*     *£250 — £350*

37 (above) A variation on the typical Edwardian Sheraton bureau of 2ft.6ins. wide dimensions in mahogany. This one has the regulation satinwood crossbanding around the mahogany surfaces but has only one drawer beneath the fall and cupboard doors containing a shelf in place of the normal two lower drawers — hence less desirable, since it is less like the original 18th century piece from which it was copied, even if it may be more useful for some people's application.

*1900-1910*                    *£200 — £300*

38 A mahogany small bureau — 2ft. wide — with splayed bracket feet in the Hepplewhite manner. Like several types of Edwardian bureau, it incorporates 'automatic action', which means that the lopers to support the fall slide out automatically when the fall is lowered. This obviates the need to pull them out manually and individually and is a security measure against lowering the fall without having the lopers extended, thus risking smashing the fall off at the hinges. Ah, progress!

*1900-1910*                    *£100 — £200*

39 (right) A figured mahogany veneered bureau in late 18th century style. A very faithful reproduction in terms of proportion and restraint, with only the matched veneers on the drawers giving away perhaps the late origins of its manufacture.

*1910-1930*                    *£350 — £550*

40 (left) A carved oak bureau which is characteristic in production and style. The lion-mask carved drawer handles are characteristic and the carving of the fall draws on 17th century models but adds 19th century arrangement to it. Note the solid frieze of the base — no concession to history there.

*1895-1915*                    *£250 — £350*

41 (right) Another carved oak bureau with 'lion-mask' handles, this time on bracket feet but with the typical Edwardian addition of a shelf on top with a carved cresting rail.

*c.1900*                    *£275 — £400*

43 (left) A walnut bureau 2ft.6ins. wide on feet which are half-way between Hepplewhite splayed feet and cabrioles. Otherwise unexceptional.

*1920-1930*                    *£100 — £200*

42 This is not a contemporary oak bureau. It is an 18th century bureau which has been carved up by a Victorian 'medievaliser' or creator of 'antiques'. Covered over with a penetrating black stain and carved with 17th century forms, the piece met the taste for medieval oak popular at the turn of the century.

*1895-1915 for the carving*
*£500 — £700*

44 (right) The end of the line in bracket feet. An oak bureau which is not reproduction as such and yet owes much to traditional design. The attempt to modify the traditional bracket foot into a tapered version is not successful. The slightly art deco metal embellishment on the fall and the feet are all that distinguish the piece from a standard type.

*c.1930*                    *£60 — £90*

# BUREAUX — reproduction, on legs

This section covers several types of bureaux which emulate earlier styles with varying degrees of accuracy. They are mainly small pieces of furniture intended for occasional use.

45 (left) A made-up oak desk on stand with an interesting contrast of styles which works quite well. The top desk section has been carved in 17th century style and has a false drawer with two rectangular moulded panels on the front. The base is pad-footed in the style of George II, say around 1730 to 1740 and has been carved to match the top. A decorator's piece.

*1870-1890*       *£200 — £300*

46 (above right) A mahogany bureau with rather striped crossbanding, on turned legs with inverted cups of William and Mary inspiration. A combination of styles from late 17th to late 18th century which is feeble, particularly in the inlaid central motif in the fall, which is neither one thing nor t'other. To be exported joyfully.

*1900-1910*                     *£150 — £250*

47 (left) A further bureau in the Sheraton-cum-William and Mary manner made, like the previous example, in mahogany. The overall effect is thin and cheap.

*1900-1910*
*£100 — £200*

48 (above right) An oak bureau of Queen Anne inspiration in style, on tapering legs ending in pad feet. It has a lot of pigeon holes inside, two long drawers under the fall and, like many of these Edwardian pieces, is rather small — 2ft.6ins. wide.

*1900-1910*                 *£100 — £180*

49 (right) A japanned bureau of Chippendale 'design', decorated with chinoiserie features and with a pot stand on the turned cross stretchers between the legs. A decorator's piece.

*1920-1940*                                          *£300 — £450*

50 (above) A lacquer and mahogany bureau in the Queen Anne style of the 1920s, on cabriole legs. The fall front encloses a fitted interior on the lines of its early 18th century inspiration. The chinoiserie lacquer is of a type which, along with 'Queen Anne' burr walnut of many quarterings, gained a tremendous popularity in the 1920s and early 1930s. Not cheap because many would try to sell it as a period piece.

*1920-1930*                                          *£300 — £450*

51 (right) A 1920s reproduction in which both lacquer chinoiserie work and a gilt stand are combined. In emulation of something Queen Anne but, again, really a decorator's piece.

*c.1920*                                          *£300 — £450*

52 (left) A burr walnut bureau on high cabriole legs ending in pad feet. Quite clearly intended as a reproduction of a Queen Anne period piece of quality. The legs are well made and shaped from solid walnut and are carved with scroll decoration ending in slightly Adam-classical pendant leaf decoration on the knee. The squared lip moulding around the legs below the knee is a period feature. Where the departure from the original starts is in the veneers — fall and drawers much too burr, contrasting too much with the straight-grained sides and banded carcase front, and the embellished top corners (the idea for which comes from the period use of re-entrant corners), and — most telling, this — the lack of any finish to the drawer edges to relate them to the carcase edges which are cross-banded. A period piece would have those drawer edges either lip-moulded, cock-beaded or at least crossbanded themselves. The proportion of the drawers is another point — the chances are that a period piece would have only had one drawer of a shallower dimension than these, which are a little too square in proportion for the piece.

*1920-1930*                                             *£250 — £350*

53 The classic oak 'Jacobethan' bureau of the 1920s and 1930s. Raised on twist-turned legs of Restoration Stuart origin and with moulded geometric panels on the drawer fronts dating from slightly later Stuart examples. So popular that the genus was made in vast numbers and is now being avidly traded in the 'shipping goods' business to overseas buyers.

*1920-1940*                        *£90 — £160*

54 The version as the late '20s and '30s saw it — the bulbous legs retained to give a Jacobethan effect but turned with rings of modernistic type. The top has been chamfered off at the corners to give what would now be thought of as an art deco look.

*c.1930*                                *£90 — £140*

55 (left) An interesting walnut break-front bookcase. The glazed upper doors and the lower doors are decorated with an arched fretted carving in a 'naturalistic' style. In form there is not much progress from designs of the 1840s and such pieces continued to be popular until the 1880s, often making dating difficult.

*1860-1880*                     *£2,500 — £4,000*

56 (below left) A break-front bookcase of c.1840 with Gothic arching in the treatment of the glazing bars. The flattened arch of the lower doors is characteristic of the 1840s but is still to be seen in catalogues of the 1880s.

*1840-1880*                     *£1,800 — £3,000*

57 (below) A classic example of a bookcase of a design originating in the 1840s but still to be found in manufacturers' catalogues, such as Shoolbreds, as late as 1880. In mahogany, almost always.

*1840-1880*                     *£350 — £500*

58 (left) A Reformed Gothic bookcase made by Marsh & Jones, showing many of the design characteristics typical of the type. Note the sloping architectural roof, with its 'tiled' effect achieved by clinker-built planking, and its gables which even include barge-boards. It is a roof style beloved by Burges but also used by other designers. Note also the incised decoration, the 'revealed' construction with pegged tenon joints and the 'structural' pillars which are, in fact, purely decorative. Inlaid ivory and ebony decoration complete the scene.

*1860-1870*                                                                    *£3,000 — £4,000*
*(Photo: Courtesy Jeremy Cooper Ltd.)*

59 (below left) An oak revival bookcase carved with lion masks and leaves, with geometric mouldings on the doors, pillars, dentillated mouldings and many other attractions to the 'medieval' fan. In the *Price Guide to Victorian Furniture* (now defunct) it was described as mid-Victorian, but this seems very unlikely. It is almost certainly late Victorian and could even be Edwardian. This chronological correction does not make it any cheaper, however.

*c.1890*                                                                         *£1,200 — £2,000*

60 (right) A mahogany bookcase, with marquetry inlay, in the Sheraton manner, set on an 'outset' lower part which has two long drawers on four square tapering legs. The Edwardians were fond of these rather top-heavy pieces which look a little uncertain, on their slender tapering legs, of bearing the load expected of them. Sheraton and Hepplewhite used this form incorporating a cylinder bureau to the lower half. The illustrated version is nearly always 20th century.

*1900-1910*
*£400 — £650*

61 (left) A solid walnut secretaire bookcase of a type made by Norman and Stacey 1900-1910 and then available at a price of £11. 11s. 0d. It was also available in fumed oak or mahogany. The walnut used for this typical piece, with its bas-relief carved door panels and secretaire drawer, tended to be an American walnut of straight grain and reddish colour. The pediment of semi-broken type is also typical of the period and the handles are original. Note that the piece was also available without the secretaire drawer, but simply with cupboards below, for £7. 18s. 6d. The reader may note that the *Price Guide to Victorian Furniture,* published in 1973, illustrated the piece from Norman & Stacey's catalogue on page 218, and priced it at £80-£120. The above photograph is courtesy of Sotheby's Belgravia where the piece shown was sold in September 1979.

*1900-1910*                                          *£750 — £950*

62 (below left) A bigger version of the previous bookcase, with typical bas relief carving and pedimented top. Would also make a very useful kitchen dresser. No secretaire drawer, so not so highly priced.

*1900-1910*                                          *£700 — £900*

63 (below right) A carved oak bookcase with broken pediment. The doors have leaded lights instead of glazing bars, a fashion quite popular with furniture from about 1890 onwards.

*1900-1910*                                          *£750 — £900*

64 A reproduction mahogany break-front bookcase in a style of the 1790-1810 period. It is a quite faithful reproduction in proportion and in treatment of the glazing bars. This popular item of furniture for wealthy bibliophiles is still being reproduced today, 'made up' from old wood or other items by less scrupulous 'restorers' anxious to pass the piece off as old, or simply reproduced to order and size by honest manufacturers. A hardy perennial of the furniture trade.

*This example 1900-1930*      *£2,000 — £3,000*
*With marquetry £3,000 — £5,000*

65 A lesser version to follow the previous example, showing typical 'Edwardian Sheraton' characteristics in the satinwood banding around doors and drawers.

*1900-1910*      *£1,000 — £2,000*

66 (left) A 'Samuel Pepys' walnut bookcase, derived from the design made for Pepys and now in the Pepysian library at Cambridge. The glazed doors have heavily carved mouldings above and below and the cupboards below these doors are of the low proportion associated with the design.

*1900-1925*
*£750 — £1,000*

67 An oak cabinet or bookcase in the Grand Jacobethan manner on large bulbous turned and reeded legs. Complete with reeded columns down the sides, geometrically moulded and fielded panels, carved leaves, carved bunches of grapes and, to cap it all, an arcaded cavetto moulding above a dentil one.

*c.1920*      *£350 — £550*

68 A mahogany bookcase of a form used from the 1840s to nearly the end of the century. A small scrolled leaf decorates the side pillars which, in this case, are reeded. The piece stands on a plinth and the shelves are adjustable.

*1850-1880*                                      *£250 — £350*

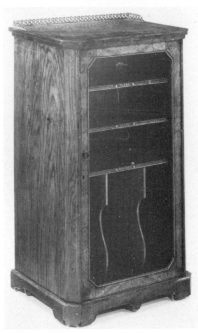

69 A walnut music cabinet of a type conforming to the more severe outline of mid-Victorian popularity. There are both shelves and fitted vertical divisions and a brass gallery rail on the top.

*1860-1880*                *£180 — £240*

70 (above) A solid walnut side cabinet or bookcase in the Gothic Reformed style, in which the lowest of the three panels in each side door is not carved for some reason. A sort of Talbert-Eastlake piece, missing its top structure, which is characteristic of the 'revealed' construction and decoration of the genre.

*c.1875*                                      *£250 — £350*

71 (right) A post-war leaded-light bookcase in the 'Jacobethan' manner, in oak of a cheap variety. Raised on twist-turned legs with square stretchers and with one applied split baluster-type decoration on the frieze.

*1920-1930*                                      *£90 — £140*

72 A bookcase or display cabinet by Gordon Russell, of 1926 date. Note the almost severe use of the latticed glazing bars — the lattice was used by Gimson and subsequently by Russell, on chairs and other furniture.

*1926*        *£250 — £450*

## CABINETS — bookcases, revolving

73 An oak bookcase of c.1930 in what would now be called an art deco style but which could in fact be traced back to pre-1914 German styles in its origins. A bureau section is lodged in an aggressively Cubist fashion into the bookcase, which has two flanking cupboards. The carved corner decoration on each door is characteristic of what is now very loosely called art deco furniture.

*c.1930*        *£30 — £60*

74 An oak revolving bookcase of typical Edwardian design, usually found in mahogany with 'Sheraton' decoration. This one is carved with leaf and floral decoration, including the top.

*1900-1920*        *£100 — £150*

75 A kingwood side cabinet decorated in the grand manner with an inlaid trellis diamond flowerhead pattern in the frieze, repeated as a decorative motif throughout. The diagonal treatment of the kingwood veneer banding around the doors and on the base is in the French manner and can be seen behind the trellis marquetry of the centre door with its glazed oval panel. There are porcelain panels painted with figures and gilt metal mounts with masks and leaf casts as additional decoration. Although it is an English piece, it has leant heavily on French inspiration and Exhibition stimulus. The curved side doors are glazed to reveal further display shelves.

*1860-1880*        *£3,000 — £5,000*

76 A walnut side cabinet with two central cupboard doors each having oval porcelain plaques painted with couples in 18th century dress. The curved side doors are glazed and reveal shelves intended for display. The frieze is also inset with porcelain oval plaques and there is a stamped gilt metal gadrooning around this frieze, the top edge of the base and the centre door edge. The central door panels also have gilt metal decoration and are symmetrically quartered with carefully-chosen veneers.

*1860-1880*        *£1,500 — £2,500*

77 A kingwood side cabinet showing 'French' diagonal treatment of the veneer figure, but with glazed doors at the centre instead of veneered panelled ones. The tops of these central doors and the curved glazed side doors, with serpentine, dipping shape is not usual on English pieces. The bun feet are ebonised and there are gilt-metal mounts throughout.

*1860-1880*        *£900 — £1,200*

78 A burr walnut side cabinet of the 'D' shaped type with burr maple banding. There is a porcelain panel in the centre door, depicting cherubs, and there are gilt-metal mounts round the edges of the frieze and on the main frame panels. The curved glazed side doors enclose curved shelves. A very popular piece of the 1870s and 1880s but originating in early sideboard-chiffonier designs of the 1850s.

1860-1890                    £1,000 — £1,500

79 Another walnut D-type side cabinet with gilt-metal mounts and porcelain panels. Very similar to the previous example but with extra gilt-metal mounting around the top edge of the base and the whole piece jacked up on turned feet. The top does not have a moulded edge, nor does the base, and there is less panelled decoration in the veneering. There also appears to be less variation in the figure and burr of the walnut.

1860-1890                    £800 — £1,200

80 A fully ebonised side cabinet with serpentine glazed doors either side enclosing shelves with shot-silk lining. The piece is inlaid with boxwood stringing and has gilt-metal mounts throughout. The centre door has a porcelain panel. It would be tempting to associate this jet black furniture with the death of Prince Albert in 1861, after which Victoria herself wore the colour, but the revived use of ebonising probably followed the great Exhibitions, particularly that of Paris in 1855 — great French cabinet makers were not known as *ébénistes* for nothing. The commercial catalogues of the 1870s and 1880s show, however, that such pieces must have continued in popularity for a long time. Definitely now a specialised taste — the market does not like black.

1875-1890                    £500 — £800

82 An ebonised Aesthetic Movement cabinet with be-spindled top gallery, mirror, fielded solid panels and painted panels of floral decoration. In the base there is a sort of 'pot board' shelf with further turned and fluted pillars at the sides. Note the small circular inlaid 'pies' at the carcase joints.

*1870-1880*
*£300 — £450*

81 A display cabinet designed by Clement Heaton with a glazed three-panel upper part and a painted lower part with scenes from Aesop's Fables. An unusual version of late Reformed Gothic work.

*c.1880*                                          *£2,500 — £2,800*

83 A very interesting ebonised and inlaid Reformed Gothic display cabinet by Gillows & Co. The pillars, with their architectural, 'roofed' bases, turned collars and ornamental capitals are of the sort of structural stonework design that one associates with the style. So is the moulded edge around the top and the brass gallery rail at the back with quatrefoil pierced design. The door hinges are of the strap, 'revealed' type but the inlays are perhaps a little bit more floral than the Reformed Gothic pieces of the early 1860s.

*c.1870*                                          *£1,000 — £2,000*

84 An ebonised inlaid side cabinet of Aesthetic Movement characteristics — spindled gallery, decorative panels, bevelled mirrors, 'pot board' shelf beneath with ring-turned columns — but, unusually, drawers inlaid with amboyna or some other burr wood. One is led to believe that this is a commercial manufacturer's version of Art Furniture, with concessions to popular taste and the fact that Edwards and Roberts, the renowned reproducers, both made and stamped it, reinforces this view.

*c.1880*                                          *£350 — £500*

85 An ebonised mahogany display cabinet of commercial design, with a rather Japanese glazing arrangement in the central doors and upswept ends to the top surfaces.

*c.1890*                                          *£200 — £300*

86 An ebonised side cabinet of mixed Aesthetic and commercial origin, with painted panels depicting an owl and a cockerel. The fluted columns and inlaid decoration are acceptable commercial practice; the spindled lower gallery and painted panels are purely Aesthetic. The lower panels are satinwood inlaid with flowers.

*1880-1890*                                      *£700 — £1,200*

87 (left) An amboyna and ebonised side cabinet showing the more severe style and increasing use of ebonising, which had both become more fashionable than the rococo plasticity of curve during the 1860s. There are three drawers in the frieze below the top which have porcelain plaques and gilt-metal bandings to decorate them. The central area has two cupboards set with porcelain plaques in the doors and an open area below, euphemistically termed a gallery. This centre section is flanked by glazed doors enclosing velvet-lined shelves. The workmanship and finish require the highest order of craftsmanship.

*1865-1880*                                      *£750 — £1,000*

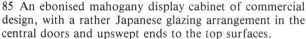

88 (right) A burr walnut and ebonised bonheur-du-jour, is included in this section because it is tempting to compare it with 87, and to speculate whether the same maker was involved in both pieces. There is the use of the two cupboards with porcelain-plaqued doors; there are the three frieze drawers with porcelain plaques and gilt-metal bandings, this time the central drawer fitted for writing. Even the burr wood panels are similarly handled, save for an extra crossband set around them. From there on the piece departs from 87, however, for the pillars are fluted and gilded — the use of turning has made them thus flashier. The top has a brass gallery rail around it and, again, the columns are turned and the fluting emphasised by gilt. 87 is more restrained. Perhaps it was simply that gilt-metal mounts, bandings and porcelain plaques all came from one manufacturing source — a sort of Beardmore's of the 1870s — so there was little choice for the cabinet maker.

*1865-1870*                                      *£1,200 — £1,800*

## CABINETS — side and display, 'art nouveau' 1890-1910

89 (left) an art nouveau mahogany display cabinet of rather flimsy construction, with stained glass decoration to the leaded glazed door and inlaid with beechwood flowers. Rather Liberty's in design but a bit more sophisticated and individual.

*c.1900*      *£200 — £350*

90 (right) an art nouveau bow-fronted display cabinet with glazed side doors decorated with leaded mauve leaves. The bowed doors are inlaid with apple tree motifs and the tapering baluster columns in the central shelf section are purely decorative.

*c.1900*      *£300 — £500*

91 An interesting side cabinet of art nouveau design of English origins, the only sinuousness perceptible being in the inlays. The use of much-leaded glazing appears to have been a feature of later English art nouveau which emulated some Arts and Crafts Movement designers. Certainly leading was used in the 1920s to give a sort of 'craft' look. The thin tapering legs are straight, not splayed in 1950s Danish fashion — the one on the left has been dislodged.

*c.1900*      *£400 — £600*

92 An art nouveau cabinet of a design possibly emanating from Liberty's, who were much associated with art nouveau furniture. The cabinet is of mahogany with inlaid decoration. Note the flat square feet like the 'caps' on art nouveau uprights and the exaggeration of the flat top.

*c.1900*      *£250 — £400*

93 (left) A side cabinet by Gardner & Son of Glasgow, in the art nouveau manner. Note the flat capped uprights, echoed by the feet. The stained glass in the glazed doors is balanced by the inlays in the solid doors, although the 'whiplash' above is not very consistent with the geometric curves below.

*c.1900*       *£200 — £300*

94 (right) An art nouveau display cabinet in mahogany with decorative inlays of floral motifs. Note, again, the flat capped uprights so favoured by Voysey and the pernickety grouping of the 'balusters' in the top gallery in threes and fives.

*c.1900*       *£600 — £900*

95 (left) A mahogany side cabinet, the design of which is the result of a union between art nouveau principles and the characteristic Edwardian upper shelf with centrally arched back, this time pierced into the ever-popular broken pediment. The result is that the top has a curiously inglenooked effect while the rest of the cabinet is conventional enough, with some art nouveau inlays.

*c.1900*       *£250 — £400*

96 (right) An interesting oak cabinet with folksy-artistic leaded glazed doors above and below, the upper ones being curtained. The central door panel has a stained glass still-life scene, depicting a steaming bowl and ladle, a drinking mug or glass, a lemon and a decanter. The author naturally supposes that the piece is intended for the storage of the makings of hot punches for winter nights but then some people will think of a drink when confronted with almost anything ...

*c.1900*       *£200 — £350*

**97 (right)** A display cabinet of art nouveau style, probably intended as a music cabinet. It is made of mahogany with boxwood and ivory inlays. The top has sinuous curves in the Continental art nouveau fashion with hearts and tulip shapes incorporated in the fretwork and carving.

*c.1890*                    *£180 — £250*

**98 (left)** Another small mahogany cabinet with art nouveau tendencies, also probably intended for music. A much simpler shape, with flat capped shaping to the top and 'whiplash' forms in the inlays.

*1890-1900*                    *£100 — £200*

**99 (left)** An oak display cabinet with 'art deco' glazing bars in typical 'rising sun' or 'wireless cabinet' pattern. The legs have a wedge-like shaping more associated with 'art nouveau' styling of earlier years than those in which this piece was made.

*1920-1930*          *£30 — £50*

**100** A display cabinet on mass-produced short 'cabriole' legs. The piece is veneered in walnut and has two curved glazed doors with simple veneered vertical bars. The shelves inside are glass. Note the silvered decoration in the fixed central panel.

*c.1930*                    *£50 — £95*

# CABINETS — side and display, 'Louis' monstrosities, 1900-1914

101 (left) This display cabinet is an example of how first class inlaying can be used on a shape which puts the piece into the 'Louis Monstrosity' section. The piece is in rosewood and might have been quite attractive had not the upper half gone completely awry and out of proportion. The two flanking curved mirrors jar hideously in the total design. A shipping goods dealer would be tempted to take the whole top off and sell the bottom half as quite an elegant sideboard.

*1890-1910*            *£300 — £400*

102 (right) An ebonised china cabinet made in cheap deal, with bevelled swerving mirrors and machined fretwork plastered all over it. Inside it has plate glass shelves. The makers describe it as a 'Louis' style, perhaps originating the famous derogatory phrase 'in the style of All the Louis!' Looking at this and the subsequent pieces, one can understand and sympathise with the obsession of Percy Wells and other designers to get back to clean, functional lines and with dust.

*1900-1914*            *£40 — £80*

104 (right) An ebonised piece described as a 'Dainty Music or China Cabinet', this time with a fashionably progressive leaded-light door.

*1900-1914*            *£50 — £80*

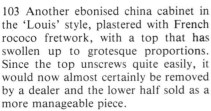

103 Another ebonised china cabinet in the 'Louis' style, plastered with French rococo fretwork, with a top that has swollen up to grotesque proportions. Since the top unscrews quite easily, it would now almost certainly be removed by a dealer and the lower half sold as a more manageable piece.

*1900-1914*        *£90 — £180*

105 Mahogany with central glazed door and chamfered glazed sides. The maker has run the front cabriole-type legs down the entire vertical height from the top shelf to the ground and secured these legs below the lower chamfered side shelf by means of an elaborate bracket. The tops of the front legs have quaint fretted brackets to secure them to the upper shelf and this eccentricity of shaping is repeated in the shelf form itself, the lower shelves — which have an odd, bitten-out centre to avoid the descending front legs — and in the absurd top which has spur-like accoutrements on the scrolled ends. When Percy Wells spoke of "flashy and flimsy furniture with embellishments and meretricious ornament", he might have had this mind. Highly destructible.

*1890-1910*        *£90 — £180*

107 (right) A rosewood inlaid side cabinet with a broken pediment above. An example of how 18th century designs returned to fashion at the end of the 19th century. Although of the 'bracket-and-overmantel' school of the late Victorian period, it would now be sold as Edwardian Sheraton due to the boxwood and ivory inlays of Adam/Sheraton inspiration.

*1890-1900     £350 — £500*

106 A late Victorian side cabinet-cum-sideboard in what has been called the 'Victorian Queen Anne' style — a term we have avoided to avert confusion because the Victorians thought that William Kent was a Queen Anne designer. Also known as the 'bracket-and-overmantel' school. It has many characteristics of the style associated with William Kent in 1720-1730 — broken pediment, reeded flat columns, classical bits, dentil frieze or mouldings, etc. Note, however, that it is made in satinwood (good grief, the expense!) and inlaid with swags and floral decoration in box or ivory and harewood, etc., a style associated with really expensive Edwardian Sheraton furniture.

*1895-1905               £1,000 — £2,000*

108 A satinwood break-front display cabinet in very 18th century style, but showing more restraint than one often associates with Edwardian reproductions. The glazing bars on the doors are in keeping and the broken pediment, with its dentilled moulding is a good proportion. The drawers are crossbanded and the side drawers additionally inlaid with oval panels. The tapering square section legs are connected by a platform stretcher and end in block feet.

*1900-1910               £2,750 — £3,750*

110 (right) A satinwood and marquetry display cabinet which is less faithful to 18th century English origins than 108, and more to Franco-Dutch ones. The serpentine shaping, dwarf cabriole legs and rather fancy broken pediment are not severe enough for the English taste and the piece is most likely to end up on the Continent. Nonetheless, a high quality reproduction in an expensive wood.

*1900-1910     £2,000 — £3,000*

109 A satinwood display cabinet in the Grand Edwardian Sheraton manner, with a moulded central glazed door and convex-glazed side doors. The decoration is all painted, relying on the 18th century for its origins, with swags, flowers, young ladies and cupids.

*1900-1910                               £1,500 — £2,000*

111 A grand form of mahogany display cabinet or bookcase incorporating many 'Chippendale' features such as a carved broken pediment on top, fretted with leaf carving of real distinction, and a carved concave top moulding. The glazing bars, in the Gothic style, are beautifully moulded and also incorporate scroll and leaf carving. The lower half has a top edge which is gadrooned and a blind fret under this top edge. The ogee or serpentine feet are carved with scrolls and bas-relief motifs of an almost Chinese inspiration. Very high quality craftsmanship required for this.

*1900-1910                   £2,000 — £4,000*

112 (left) A mahogany display cabinet with glazed door to the central cabinet and mirrored upper shelves. There are both turned and square-section tapering columns as well as turned and reeded legs. These legs and the inlays are more Adam in design than Sheraton, as are the cherubic panels.

*1900-1910*                    *£250 — £400*

113 (right) A characteristic 'Edwardian Sheraton' display cabinet with a broken pediment above. Made in mahogany with inlays and satinwood bandings and with glass shelves inside.

*1900-1914*                    *£180 — £300*

114 (below left) A walnut cabinet on twist-turned stand with crossbanded stretcher and on bun feet. There is a cushion drawer under the top moulding. This is quite a good reproduction of a piece of about 1690-1700 date but inspection of the piece in the flesh would give away the age, particularly the mouldings and the patina and type of veneer.

*c.1920*                                                    *£500 — £700*

115 (right) A chinoiserie cabinet on a gilded stand with cabriole legs ending in ball-and-claw feet. Very much reproduced in the 1920s, when the decorative qualities of chinoiserie became, once again, highly appreciated. It is, in fact, a version of an 18th century type but is quite immediately identifiable as wrong ʻo anyone familiar with the original. Why? Well, unless you're prepared to pay big money, you'll have to take my word for it, because if you don't know, you're too lazy or too mean to find out.

*1920-1940*        *£400 — £600*

# CABINETS — side and display, reproductions 1880-1930, lower

116 (left) A mahogany display cabinet, in a later version of the Edwardian Sheraton manner, on somewhat flimsy cabriole legs connected by a platform stretcher. The inlay is of stylised flowers and foliage and the top cresting shows the flattened moulded top rail so favoured at the time and derived from the art nouveau-progressive designers. A somewhat eclectic piece, now popular for china display or for collectors.

*1900-1910*          *£300 — £400*

117 (right) An inlaid mahogany display cabinet with an oval bevelled mirror above. Almost certainly a modern dealer would remove all the top mirror section and sell the glazed display cabinet as a more acceptable, rectangular piece with 18th century design associations. For this reason, this piece is included in the 'lower' cabinet section — always look carefully at the top back edge for signs of removal of upper storeys.

*1900-1914*     *With top £120 — £180*
                 *Without top £150 — £250*

118 (left) Another example of a small display cabinet which nowadays would almost certainly have the top mirror section removed and be sold as a nice, squarish, Sheraton type of cabinet.

*1900-1914*          *£80 — £120*

119 (right) A mahogany glazed display cabinet in the rococo Chippendale manner, on small thin cabriole legs ending in ball-and-claw feet. Complex to carve all that fretted work.

*c.1900*          *£350 — £500*

120 (left) A kidney-shaped display cabinet in mahogany crossbanded with satinwood in the Edwardian Sheraton manner. The top has a glazed panel with bevelled edge in it and there are husks inlaid into the stiles. The legs are a somewhat feeble gesture towards the cabriole shape but square in section and so slightly curved as to make one think that the man who made them on a band saw was not really certain what he wanted to achieve. They are neither fresh fish nor good red herring and would best have been left straight with their taper. Apart from the legs it is an elegant and desirably frivolous piece in which any lady would be pleased to display her favourite collectables — hence the price.

*1900-1910*        *£500 — £650*

121 A gilt display cabinet made of pine with gesso moulded decoration over which the gilding is carried out, like a picture frame. The style is an elegant adaptation of late 18th century classical forms.

*1900-1910*        *£400 — £550*

123 A mahogany side cabinet, of 'Chippendale' type, with a blind fret on the upper frieze and a gadrooned top edge. There are Chinese scenes in the decorated panels and the serpentine bracket feet have gadrooned top edges.

*c.1920*        *£200 — £400*

122 (above) An Adam style satinwood cabinet or commode of half-round (or *demi-lune*) shape on tapered turned feet. The painted decoration of swags and paterae and leaves and ribbons and all the paraphernalia of Adam type is there to supplement the central oval panels painted with dishevelled maidens of Angelica Kauffmann type — oh, one could go on and on, boring the reader for ever. It's an early 20th century copy of an 18th century piece and, if you're really interested, you'll read the relevant literature on the 18th century.

*1910-1920*        *£2,000 — £3,000*
*Does that whet your interest? Then make an effort to learn . . .*

# CABINETS — side, court cupboards, buffets and the like

124 (right) A high quality inlaid side cabinet by Collinson & Lock, the makers who you'll recall (that is, if you've been reading this book and not just looking at pictures) are celebrated for making the cabinet designed by T.E. Collcutt and reputedly setting off the whole Art or Aesthetic furniture craze. In this case they have produced a version of a medieval court cupboard or buffet of irritatingly little practical use, presumably intended for a hall or similar passage. One can not refute the quality of the ivory inlaid floral work, nor the crisp spiral reeding of the bold columns but what the blazes would one use it for? The plinth is somewhat lame compared with the much-moulded top which has access for storage (of gloves? a croquet set? bicycle lamps?) via the small canted side panels or the central, hinged panel. All one can say is that it is an extremely expensive way of constructing two shelves.

c.1880                                              £1,500 — £2,000
*(Oh yes, it's Collinson & Lock, you see)*
*Photo: Courtesy Jeremy Cooper Ltd.*

125 (below) An oak 'court cupboard' incorporating features which no period court cupboard would ever have known, particularly the matched oak veneering of the panelled surfaces. The raised and carved rectangular panels on the doors and the diamond-shaped panel on the upper central section are a reproducer's fancy. The turnings are a modern interpretation and so is the abundance of dentillated mouldings round the drawers and doors. (Dentil moulding is allowed on late 18th century top mouldings of court cupboards.)

1910-1930                                          £120 — £200

126 An oak court cupboard of modern treatment applied to a traditional form. The turned baluster 'supports' to the top tier are unhappily isolated against the very modern plain flat panels and drawer front of the rest of the piece. They do not relate to the feet, either, which are derived from six-plank chests of the 17th century, formed by the continuation of the sides down in a shaped apron.

1920-1930                                          £50 — £100

# CANTERBURIES

The name Canterbury comes from a piece of mobile furniture liked by one of the archbishops. Several pieces of mobile furniture fell under this category, including a supper trolley, atlas stand and the now-accepted music stand which virtually defines the breed.

The music Canterbury appeared around 1800 and was a restrained piece of mahogany furniture. The post-1860 examples illustrated here exhibit the exuberant rococo designs and other fancies of the time. Like their earlier counterparts, they tend to be relatively expensive pieces when assessed against the workmanship involved in them.

127 A burr walnut Canterbury of a kidney shape with scrolled fretwork divisions below and a pierced brass gallery rail around the top.

*c.1860*    *£400 — £650*

128 (left) A walnut Canterbury with a top which lifts to form a writing slope. The divisions below are fretted with scrolled designs.

*c.1860*    *£250 — £400*

129 (right) A walnut Canterbury with fretted naturalistic design divisions and a circular panel painted with a scene depicting a bird and flowers.

*c.1860*    *£250 — £400*

130 (left) A papier mâché music Canterbury decorated with shell and mother-of-pearl inlays. A high quality version valued for its uniquely Victorian character.

*c.1860*    *£350 — £500*

131 (right) A bamboo Canterbury of a type made from about 1880 onwards. Painted decoration in panels is frequently to be found on these pieces.

*1880-1910*    *£40 — £70*

# CHAIRS — bentwood

133 (right) A bentwood armchair of Thonet production itemised as No. 20 in the Thonet catalogue. An elegant chair of pleasant proportions.

*c.1860*      *£40 — £65*

132 Bentwood furniture was introduced to England by the Austrian, Michael Thonet, at the Great Exhibition of 1851. His rocking chair, shown here, is one of the most popular forms and has been much reproduced.

*c.1860*      *£60 — £120*

134 (left) A plain bentwood chair, catalogued as No. 14 by Thonet, and his best selling item at nearly fifty million since 1859. As used in cafés throughout Europe. During the 1870s Thonet was said to be turning out 1,200 of this model daily — see Gillian Walkling, *Antique Collecting,* December 1979.

*c.1860*      *£5 — £10*

135 (right) An unusual, high, bentwood office chair, adjustable in height and with a revolving seat. The circular seat is impressed with the pattern one associates with bentwood furniture.

*1900-1920*      *£70 — £95*

## CHAIRS — balloon back, Victorian

The balloon back chair was quite a perennially popular form and has been appreciated by collectors since the 1960s. It is worth reiterating that most balloon back chairs were not intended as dining chairs, which are structurally heavier. The light, cabriole-leg balloon back was for occasional use in the drawing or sitting room.

136 (right) A standard Victorian mahogany chair of a type made from the 1840s to the 1880s. Not actually a balloon back but showing how it could easily come about as a sequence of this design. The legs are a bit pumpkin-like and the top rail is heavy.

*1840-1880*                     *In sets, each £70 — £90*

137 (far right) A mahogany balloon back chair with some carving appended under the top rail. It would probably have been wiser to restrain this sort of decoration to the lower rail, since the appended upper carving detracts.

*1840-1880*                     *In sets, each £70 — £90*

138 (left) A classic example of an oval walnut balloon back chair with a wool-work covered seat. The amount of carving on the back and on the 'knee' of the cabriole legs, which end in scrolled feet, is restrained and pleasant.

*1850-1880*          *In sets of six or more, each £120 — £160*

139 (right) A late, turned-leg version of the balloon back in mahogany, with a central carved splat instead of a horizontal rail. The back is quite attractive but the legs, with their rather clumsy collars, the large upper ones carved with vaguely leaf forms, are not harmonious with the curves of the back.

*1850-1880*                     *In sets, each £60 — £80*

140 (below left) A variant of the balloon back on cabriole legs but with Gothic influence in the shaping of the back. The dot-dash grooving in the flat surface and the sudden cranks in the shaping are tell-tale characteristics of the later varieties of Victorian rococo.

*1850-1880*                     *In sets, each £80 — £100*

141 (below) A mahogany variation on the principle, this time with a French Louis XV shape to the back, which is upholstered. Still rococo enough for Victorian tastes and of a shape which is a perennial favourite. Sometimes known as 'French Hepplewhite'.

*1860-1880*
*In sets, each £80 — £100*

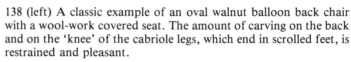

142 (right) An oval upholstered chair with a buttoned back, painted and decorated with carving. Again a French design which returned to popularity in the 1870s, conveying an impression of lightness and elegance whilst still being stronger structurally than the cabrioled balloon back. The oval back is perhaps a little heavy.

*1870-1890*
*In sets, each £90 — £100*

# CHAIRS — straight front legs, Victorian

Chairs with straight front legs in this section are generally dining chairs but, obviously, occasional chairs of this type exist as well. The variation in style is greater and most of the major schools of influence had their effect on the dining chair. Indeed, the almost sacred aura connected with the business of eating made this imperative — dining rooms were sometimes larger and more carefully furnished than sitting rooms. This is consistent with an ecclesiastical work ethic, which advised that one should be either working — out of the house or in a study — or eating, or sleeping but not idling about in a sitting room frittering away one's time.

143 (right) A mahogany chair of a design made from the 1830s to the end of the 1850s, from which this example dates. Its form clearly gave rise to many variations in back and legs but was essentially the basic upright Victorian chair's original.

*1850-1860*                                    *In sets, each £80 — £90*

144 (left) Another mid-19th century design in oak which persisted in various alternatives until later in the century. C. and R. Light illustrate an upholstered chair with a similar back in their 1887 catalogue. The desire for a vaguely medieval form is evidently satisfied by the caned panels and carved decoration.

*1840-1880*                    *In sets, each £50 — £80*

145 (right) An oak chair, described as being 'in the Eastlake manner' due to the spindled arched gallery in the back, but with slab-like front legs connected to the back ones with rather nicely-turned, baluster-formed stretchers. Acorn finials and 'money' pattern carving decorate the uprights.

*1870-1890*                    *In sets, each £60 — £80*

146 (right) Another oak chair with an arched spindled gallery in the back and a panel, strangely turned with concentric rings. The front legs are turned with a multiplicity of collars. Again, the influence of Eastlake, Talbert — any 'reformers' will do.

*1870-1890*
*In sets, each £30 — £50*

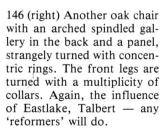

147 (left) Another oak chair with turned spindled galleries, of a type popular in the 1870s and 1880s. This is the armchair out of a dining set using single chairs of similar design. The triangular top rail is carved in bas-relief with floral scrolls and the leather covered upholstery has a Prince of Wales' feathers motif on the back.

*1870-1890*
*In sets, each £40 — £60*

148 An interesting 'near pair' of chairs of very high quality. There is an aura of the Aesthetic Movement about the spindled galleries but the quality of turning and the latticing of the back of the right-hand version lead one to feel that one of the celebrated designers may have had a hand in them, Godwin perhaps, for there is an Anglo-Japanese feel to them, or even Norman Shaw, who designed similar chairs for Lord Armstrong's house, Cragside. In fact, they are by Waterhouse, an architect who designed furniture for a manufacturer called Capeland, and was a close friend of Norman Shaw.

*1870-1880*　　　　　　　　　　　　　　　*Set of six £1,500 — £2,500*

149 An occasional chair in mahogany, of a design found in manufacturers' catalogues of the 1870s and 1880s with incised, or 'scratch', decoration. Usually part of a suite of chaise-longue, armchairs and six singles, akin to balloon backs.

*1870-1880*
*In sets of six or more, each £50 — £60*

150 Another similar chair of lighter construction, incised with dot-dash grooving and inlaid with boxwood motifs.

*1870-1880*
*In sets, each £50 — £60*

151 A 'Gothic' design of oak chair made by Shoolbred. Not a happy termination to the top rail which leaves the outsides chopped off in mid air.

*1880-1890*
*In sets, each £50 — £60*

152 An oak dining chair, the 'carver' from a set of singles, of rather elaborately carved design using leaves and flowers, gadrooning and scrolls, intended to impress with the owner's importance.

*1870-1890*
*In sets, each £80 — £100*

153 Another 'grand' chair in mahogany of semi-medieval design with leatherette or rexine covering to the upholstered parts. A popular style from the 'Abbotsford' influences onwards.

*1880-1890*
*As a single armchair £80 — £100*
*A set of two plus four singles*
*£600 — £900*

154 A late, straight, 19th century chair with a needlework covering and ring-incised, turned front legs.

*1880-1890     In sets, each £40 — £60*

155 Another simple, straight chair with a spindled gallery and ringed front legs.

*1880-1890     In sets, each £20 — £40*

## CHAIRS — reproductions, 1880-1930

The return to 18th century styles in the 1880s affected chairs almost more than other furniture. Chippendale, Sheraton and Hepplewhite chairs were produced in varying grades of quality and exactitude. Queen Anne cabriole legs with 'fiddle' backs soon followed and, of course, the medieval oak craze had to be met by chair makers . . .

156 (left) A mahogany 'Chippendale' chair of some considerable quality. The carved splat is of Gothic style in its origins and the scrolled cabriole legs end in ball-and-claw feet. It is still unmistakably Victorian, however, from its slightly narrow proportions.

*1880-1900*
*In sets, each £100 — £140*

157 (right) A highly-carved 'Chippendale' chair with a wool-work tapestry seat. The narrow proportions, particularly of the back, proclaim it to be Victorian. The cabriole legs, which are elegantly carved, show that incipient bandyness and weakness at the ankle which are also characteristic.

*1880-1900*
*In sets, each £100 — £150*

158 (left) A mahogany 'Chippendale' chair with a back of quite faithful reproduction. The seat is, however, smaller than the original would have been and the seat rail has been made the same width as the legs. The original would have been more likely to have a deeper seat rail even if the legs were of the same proportions.

*1880-1900*                    *In sets, each £70 — £100*

159 (right) A mahogany 'Chippendale' ladderback chair with carved pierced rails to the back, which is well executed. The seat and the square legs are, again, small and thin compared with the 18th century original; the seat rail is not deep enough.

*1880-1900*                    *£80 — £100*

160 (below left) Typical mass-produced 'Chippendale' style chairs with rexine (imitation leather) covered drop-in seats. No problems of confusion with the originals here; both 'carvers' and single chairs are of proportion and dimensions well away from the 18th century. The Gothic style back splat is quite a good copy of an original design.

*1890-1930*
*In sets, each £40 — £70*

161 (right) A mahogany 'Hepplewhite' chair of very good proportion, on moulded square tapering front legs. The back is a variation of the shield back, curved in shape with carving on the rails. The seat is full and bold, serpentine-shaped at the front and worthy of the original.

*1880-1900*        *£90 — £120*

162 (right) A classic shield-back 'Hepplewhite' chair with carved Prince of Wales' feathers in the back design. The tapering square legs and slightly bowed seat are copied faithfully from the original and the proportion is good. A well-made chair like this was very much more expensive than a mass-produced, thin 'Chippendale' design — about nine guineas for this as against one and a half for the mass-produced item.

*1890-1920*                    *In sets, each £60 — £100*

163 (left) A mahogany wheel-back 'Hepplewhite' chair of good proportion and workmanship. The carving of the back is a considerable achievement and, with wear, and without sight of the unpolished areas, such chairs can be difficult to tell from an original period chair.

*1890-1920, but could be made even now*
*— at a price*
*In sets, each £100 — £180*

164 A mahogany arm chair in Sheraton style with inlaid boxwood stringing lines as decoration. There is also an inlaid oval satinwood and marquetry panel in the broad top rail. These panels were available ready-made by machine from the trade.

*1890-1910*　　*In sets, each £70 — £90*

165 Not quite Sheraton and not quite Edwardian 'own brand', these small chairs still owe more to the late 18th and early 19th century than to the 1900-1910 period in which they were made. The back is a Sheraton design-book copy and the tapering square legs end in block feet.

*1890-1910*

*In sets, each £30 — £50*

166 An example of the mahogany 'Queen Anne' style of dining chair which had a great vogue from around 1900 to 1940. They do not seek to emulate original Queen Anne period chairs too closely — these examples are usually mahogany or stained to look like it, and mahogany was not used in quantity until after 1730 — and they are mass-produced in unmistakably economic ways, so there is little problem in differentiating them from the originals.

*1900-1940*　　*In sets, each £30 — £50*

167 Elegant mahogany chairs based on a Queen Anne design and of a shape quite popular in the early 20th century. The front legs are an English variation on the cabriole, usually associated with country makers. The back curves are restrained without being stiff. The central panel of the back is caned and the pin-cushion seat is covered with a striped tapestry. Intended as an occasional chair but would now be sold for dining.

*1900-1920*　　*In sets, each £35 — £55*

168 Typical 'Jacobean' chairs, in oak, of a type also very popular from 1890-1940, made to go with the bulbous-legged refectory-style table of the 'Jacobethan' dining room. Twist turning is the key to these chairs which owe their form to the second half of the 17th century.

*1890-1940*              *In sets, each £40 — £60*

169 (right and below) Four more variations on the popular 'Jacobean' chair theme, with pincushion seats covered in rexine (an imitation leather). More expensive than the previous examples because the stretchers between the legs are turned as well, not just left square for cheapness. The pair on the right have abandoned the twist turning normally used and have turned pillar supports capped by finials instead. (The rather elaborately carved top rail was not popular on post-1920 versions.)

*1890-1920*              *In sets, each £30 — £60*

E 843

170 (right) The end of the line for the 'Jacobethan' style. An oak chair with twist turning in prominent places and cheap square sections elsewhere. The drop-in seat is covered in rexine.

*1920-1930*
*In sets, each £10 — £20*

171 An oak arm and a single chair in 'Carolean' style with caned back and seat panels. They are fairly faithful reproductions of chairs of the Restoration period of 1680-1690, showing the elaborately-carved scrolled front stretcher between the front legs echoed in the top rail of the high back. They would be detected by the lack of age and wear apparent in them, and by their colour. Such chairs were originally made of birch, beech, oak or walnut and stained black. They are very decorative but not popular as dining chairs due to the weakness of the seat jointing to the back and legs; the very thinness of the seat frame makes the joints very susceptible to breakage by weight or leverage. Nevertheless, this design, of all reproductions, is probably the one most faithfully copied.

*1890-1930*            *Each £150 — £250*

173 (right) An oak chair of square design in emulation of the 1650-1670 period and often known as 'Cromwellian'. The turning on the front legs is not of a period type.

*1890-1920*
*In sets, each £60 — £80*

172 (above) A pair of oak bobbin-turned chairs in the style of 1660-1680 with leather covered backs and seats, peppered with large brass-headed studs like a pair of Restoration Hell's Angels! These must surely have met the taste for medievalism with a vengeance. The bobbin-turned stretchers and the legs, with their square-section joints, look like faithful copies of the originals.

*1880-1930*            *In sets, each £60 — £80*

174 (right) Another pair of oak chairs, known as Cromwellian in style, which emulate those of 1650-1670. They are similar to the previous examples but the more severe column turning of the legs, with plain square stretchers joining them at ground level, is perhaps more apposite to the Protector's time. Covered in velvet and just right for that big reproduction refectory table in the dining room.

*1890-1930*            *In sets, each £60 — £80*

175 (right) A 'Queen Anne' style chinoiserie chair of considerable quality. There was a revival of lacquer of this type in the 1920s and 1930s, with some high quality 'reproductions', in somewhat free interpretations, being produced.

*1920-1930     For the single armchair £80 — £120*
*A set of two plus four singles £450 — £700*

176 (left) A reproduction of a caned French chair which, in Britain, has connotations of Adam and other classical styles. The chair is gilded over a gesso surface and has, unfortunately, an air of belonging to a ballroom or dining room of an old-fashioned hotel.

*1890-1940          In sets, each £40 — £60*

## CHAIRS — small Edwardian oak

177 The period from 1900 to 1914 saw the mass production of a large number of small chairs of rather square proportion, made in oak. Some had drop-in seats, some were rushed, some simply webbed and upholstered with a shiny rexine covering. Their design was quite simple and functional; the legs were either square section tapering or turned and the back, fairly severe in outline, leant sometimes to the 18th century and sometimes to more modern, art nouveau designs for its style. Individual comment on each version would be either un-rewarding or unwise. Suffice it to say that they are still a source of cheap matched seating. The selection below and on the opposite page shows a small part of the total variations that were made.

*1900-1914                                    In sets, each £10 — £20*

# CHAIRS — Arts and Crafts, Art Nouveau and after : 1860-1930

The reader is not going to be bored by another harangue on the differences between the Arts and Crafts Movement and Art Nouveau. That is done frequently throughout other sections of the book. Most of the chairs here will be known loosely as 'art nouveau' by the trade and many collectors. So be it.

We have illustrated a chair by Charles Rennie Mackintosh for information even though many would claim that it should not be in a Guide of this sort. We dispute this hotly as we explained in the Introduction. Although chairs by Mackintosh are perhaps the province of Sotheby's Belgravia and other fine art specialists when it comes to sale values, this book is used as much as an art reference work as it is a Price Guide. Besides, our readers are not beyond finding a Mackintosh chair and an indication of value is what they are paying for.

178 (above right) A William Morris rush-seated 'Sussex' armchair as shown in the firm's catalogues of the 1870s. This chair is also featured in the Country and Kitchen section but it is legitimately shown here because the middle-class trendies who bought Morris & Co. furniture used these chairs for dining and occasional use, thus reflecting the genuine role that Morris & Co. played in the Arts and Crafts Movement. Many rush-seated chairs were produced in emulation of this precedent. So there!

*1865-1895*                          *Singly £55 — £70   In sets, each £60 — £80*

179 A rush-seated chair by William Burges (q.v.) painted dark green, with painted decoration. It has been remarked (by Michael Whiteway) that the chair looks like something out of a modern Italian café. Possibly slightly pre-dates the William Morris chairs but at this point Burges and Morris were fairly close.

*c.1865*
*£150 — £220*
*(because by Burges)*

180 (left) The celebrated design by A.H. Mackmurdo of the Century Guild. A chair with a high back and original upholstery with characteristic 'heart' shapes. A similar chair is in the Victoria and Albert Museum.

*c.1885*                          *£300 — £400*

181 (right) Another chair by the William Morris firm, in which the tulip motif has been used in the inlaid panels in the back uprights. Again, based on a traditional form but this time the width of the back and the length of the arms is a bit attenuated.

*1900-1912*                          *£90 — £120*

182 (right) The use of rush seating seems to have been an almost morally-inspired move by the members of the Arts and Crafts Movement, as though rush seats and plain oak, with their 'country' connotations, were somehow less decadent than stuffed Victorian upholstery. But then architects have always been puritans at heart. Add to that characteristic the socialist principles of William Morris and where do you land? On something fairly hard, usually. It was Voysey and others, designing in what is known as the 'vernacular' tradition, i.e. in the native idiom — who produced chairs in clean lines made of plain oak and with seats of rush. This chair exhibits all these characteristics and the motifs, now associated with 'art nouveau', such as the heart shape, used by Voysey.

*1890-1910*                          *If attributable to a known designer, £100 — £140*
*If not, £40 — £60*

184 (left) An oak rush-seated chair in a style going on from progressive-art nouveau towards something more modern, as evidenced by the arched cross-stretcher between the legs. The tapering back with the pierced 'handle' looks most uncomfortable.

*1905-1915*
*In sets, each*
*£20 — £30*

185 (right) More rush seating, more vertical discomfort. Very much a 'clean' architect's design, the back following a model by William Birch.

*c.1900*
*In sets,*
*each £20 — £30*

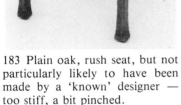

183 Plain oak, rush seat, but not particularly likely to have been made by a 'known' designer — too stiff, a bit pinched.

*1980-1910*
*In sets each, £25 — £35*

186 (right) Chair designed by Charles Rennie Mackintosh of Glasgow, now famous for the elongated shape, the low proportion of the seat and the strange motifs, weepy eyes, seagulls-viewed-end-on and other Mackintosh hallmarks. Before you mock or turn away, reflect that Mackintosh designed his furniture to make specific impacts in rooms of high proportion or in the now-famous cafés and tea rooms where other designs would have been unnoticed. His work now sells as 'art' rather than furniture, hence the price.

*1890-1910*                    *£2,500 — £3,500*

187 An art nouveau armchair with decorated back panel in characteristic floral design. The wavy arm supports are a 'quaint' feature. Possibly Liberty's. May have had a rush seat subsequently covered over.

*c.1900*                    *£80 — £95*

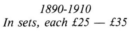

188   A more commercial art nouveau chair with characteristic heart shapes cut through. The seat looks like a repair job.

*c.1900*               *£20 — £35*

189   Commercial oak chair with a rexine or leatherette seat cover fixed by brass studs. Owing something to 'art nouveau' styles due to the tapering back and legs ending in 'block' feet but fairly mass-produced in appearance.

*1890-1910*
*In sets, each £25 — £35*

190   Another oak art nouveau chair, quite good quality and stiffened for strength by the curved apron under the seat. An enduring design.

*c.1900*
*In sets, each £20 — £30*

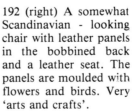

192 (right) A somewhat Scandinavian - looking chair with leather panels in the bobbined back and a leather seat. The panels are moulded with flowers and birds. Very 'arts and crafts'.

*c.1900*      *£100 — £140*

191 Arm and single chair of commercial production with drop-in rush seats.

*c.1900*            *Singles in sets, each £20 — £30*
*arm, each £35 — £45*

193 (right) A lattice-back chair by Ernest Gimson. He was fond of the lattice back and many who admired him followed this feature. Note that the chair is deceptively simple; it is beautifully made and carefully thought out. The box-and-ebony stringing lines inlaid in the back uprights are characteristic of the later Arts and Crafts Movement.

*c.1915*                    *Set of six £2,000 — £3,000*
*Photo: Courtesy Jeremy Cooper Ltd.*

194 (left) Another lattice back, this time by Ambrose Heal, in oak. A very traditional, almost 18th century chair. As it is a furnisher's chair, the seat has been upholstered and covered in a contemporary material, rather than the rush seat of Gimson type.

*1910-1920*                    *Set of six £1,000 — £2,000*
*Photo: Courtesy Michael Whiteway*

195 (left and below left) More 'Cotswold' lattice back chairs, this time with leather seats and cabriole/pad foot front legs.

*1910-1920*                                        *Set £500 — £1,000*

196 Three chairs with wooden seats and loose cushions from Percy Wells, c.1920, intended for 'the small house' or cottage. The design is an interesting blend of simple sub-18th century lower halves, combined with top halves that are also derived from the 18th century and art furniture. Wells disapproved of all the modern chairs in "tens of thousands of cottages and small houses in the streets of our towns and cities". He must have been busier than a church visitor. The only good examples, to him, were Windsors, stick, or ladderback types, but — wait for it — they were not 'easy to dust'. Deplorably, people would think of Windsors as kitchen chairs and would hence buy stuffed-seat plush chairs with a little bad carving on the back and, still worse, polishing or varnishing the legs. Wells' designs aimed at being strong, comfortable and easy to clean. They were made in any hard wood such as oak, elm, beech or birch, and were intended to strike a medium between 'kitchen' chairs and 'flashy and flimsy' modern chairs. They were pretty successful in meeting his objectives and survive in large numbers, with variants in the back design. Not far removed from the small oak Edwardian chairs illustrated earlier, but far better in proportion and design.

*c.1920*                                        *In sets, each £10 — £20*

197 A mahogany 'carving' chair designed by Percy Wells c.1920. The legs and arms are distinctly Sheraton in form but the ladder-back is much more forceful and owes something to the Heal-Gordon Russell school of design.

*c.1920* £35 — £55

198 (above) Good fan-back dining chairs, of 18th century inspiration, of a type made in walnut, oak or mahogany. An honest simple design which is again thin below the seat — the front seat rail would look much better if it were deeper.

*1920-1930* *In sets, each £20 — £40*

199 (right) An oak chair with a 'sunburst' back — art deco is on the way. An otherwise unremarkable chair except for the thoughtful chamfering of the square front legs at the edges.

*1910-1920* *In sets, each £20 — £30*

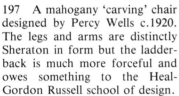

200 Lattice-back chairs of the 1920s, made in oak walnut or mahogany. Probably inspired by the Ernest Gimson-Gordon Russell school of lattice backs but in this case from Maurice Adams. Actually these examples by Adams are well-proportioned, if a bit severe, and their modernity is in an 18th century tradition, whereas Gimson, in one of his lattice-backs, terminated the square section front legs in little, scrolled feet, which must have set even his most ardent followers' teeth on edge.

*1920-1930* *Depending on identification £30 — £70*

201 An interesting design of oak chair, showing the arm, or 'carver' and single chair from a set. The back, with its simple cross-lattice, reflects influences going back to Russell, Gimson and even Godwin, but the arms are not particularly attractive. The aforementioned designers would not have approved either of the incised carving on the top rail and the front legs, introduced by a commercial manufacturer to give more popular appeal to a rather severe design.

*c.1930* *In sets, each £10 — £15*

# CHAIRS — country and kitchen : rush-seated, 1860-1930

We have started this section off with the William Morris Sussex rush-seated chair — again. This is appropriate, because the chair was a genuine country type 're-discovered' by the Morris firm and typical of country work which had continued uninterrupted by the vagaries of fashion. Many of the chairs in this section are of typical country type or mass-produced simple chairs suitable for kitchens and the dining room. They are reasonably durable, suitably-priced, very functional in design and mostly pleasing to look at.

202 (right) This chair may be seen on the right-hand side of the William Morris catalogue advertising the 'Sussex' range of rush-seated chairs. Originally they were birch, ebonised or stained dark green, using Ford Madox Brown's discovery of a green stain. The design of the chair is said to be traditional, and it is stronger than it looks. The posture required of the sitter is a bit severe. Note the way that the inclined arm supports go right through the seat rail and down into an extra cross stretcher, where their finely-tapered ends locate through the stretcher, like dowels, to add to strength. These chairs set a fashion for many other rush-seated types.

*1865-1895*

*Singly £55 — £70*
*In sets, each £60 — £80*

203 (left) A variation on the previous design, using the same arm-support extension down through to an extra cross-stretcher. The back design is a variant on the 'wavy-line' ladder-back.

*c.1870*

*Singly £55 — £70*
*In sets, each £60 — £80*

204 (left) A bamboo rush-seated chair in which the influence of William Morris, the Arts and Crafts Movement and the Japanese or 'quaint' style are gaily intermingled. By the 1870s, leading firms were producing bamboo furniture cheaply to cater for the popular Japanese vogue. In this chair the traditions of Sussex and Tokyo have been determinedly blended.

*1870-1910*                          *£20 — £35*

206 (below right) A fruitwood chair designed by Ernest Gimson. The rush seat is conventional. Note the careful proportion and the spacing of the ladder back — a very satisfying chair to look at.

*1880-1910*
*£150 — £220*

205 (left) Not all country chairs were made by simple country craftsmen. This oak armchair with rush seat was probably designed by R. Norman Shaw about 1876 and retailed by William Morris. It rests at the Victoria and Albert Museum, who note that it was at the Tabard Inn, Bedford Park. The high back, with turned uprights and simple straight splat, owes a good deal to early 18th century chairs, but the turning on the front legs is much later in concept.

*c.1876*                          *£120 — £200*

207 (left) A cleaned-off rush-seated arm-chair with an unusual back incorporating wavy, slightly 'quaint' slats with pierced circles in them. Made of birch and originally stained black.

*c.1885*              *£65 — £85*

208 (right) A rush-seated 'art nouveau' chair with round-capped uprights to the back which are echoed by the front legs. Although it looks simple, it is a deceptive chair, in which the plain oak surface in the back has a simple fielded panel carved in it and the spacing of the flat cross slats beneath has been very carefully designed and proportioned. It is a chair of traditional country ancestry but redesigned in a modern, arts and crafts form which indicates an architect behind it somewhere.

*1890-1910*           *£50 — £80*
*(If by 'known' architect designer, then £150 — £200)*

209 A chair by Liberty's of London of rather solid oak splat construction in the 'art nouveau' manner.

*c.1900*              *£60 — £90*

210 (right and above right) Four small rush-seated chairs of mass-produced type in sub-Sheraton designs which were intended for kitchen or dining room use. A large variety of this type were turned out in Edwardian times.

*1900-1920*          *In sets, each £10 — £25*

211 (left) A bobbin-turned yew chair with rush seat designed by Ernest Gimson. The bobbin-turning dates back to the 17th century and the style is derivative of that earlier period. Evidence again of the late 19th and early 20th century desire to get back to simpler and more natural styles.

*c.1905*                              *£180 — £250*

212 (right) A remarkable example of a low-backed ladderback chair with rush seat illustrated by Maurice Adams in 1926. The distinctive top rail is derived from the 'Macclesfield' design of country chair originating in 1790-1830. It is almost a faithful reproduction but the back design is not quite true. Would probably be sold nowadays as an 'early 19th century' chair.

*1920-1930*                    *In sets, each £40 — £70*

213 (right) A rush-seated ladderback chair of a mass-produced type, post-First War, which has used the fashion set by Morrisian and country chairs for its design. Compared with architect-designed types, it does not quite come off because the back is a little too long and clumsy, with its square uprights set at an uncomfortable angle, for the turned front legs. Nevertheless, made in a pleasant birch or beech, a cheerful chair for 'country' style kitchens or dining rooms.

*1920-1935*
*In sets, each £20 — £30*

214 (above) Quite elegant ladderback rush-seated chairs of a design not far from Ernest Gimson and traditional types but, in fact, modern chairs from Maurice Adams 1926 catalogue.

*1920-1940*                              *Arm £30 — £45*
*In sets, single £20 — £30*

215 (right) The spindle and ladderback country chair was also made throughout the 19th century and much reproduced in the 1920s and 1930s when both types suited the vogue for oak 'Jacobean' dining rooms. Both these examples are straightforward copies of early 19th century chairs taken from Maurice Adams' 1926 catalogue. There were many producers of such chairs. On the left is a spindle-back rush-seated chair of a Lancashire or Yorkshire type made from the 18th century onwards. On the right a 'wavy-line' ladderback of similar dating. Both are popular country chairs and have continued to be sought after. It is likely that many 20th century versions, with a bit of wear knocked into them, would be sold as being of much earlier date.

*1920-c.1940*                    *In sets, each £30 — £70*

# CHAIRS — country and kitchen : wooden seated, 1860-1930

This section also includes chairs for institutional and office use, made in large quantities by mass-production methods. On the whole they are more durable than rush-seated chairs and tend to be perennially favourite types such as the Windsor which is still going strong. In the mid- and late 19th century large quantities of simple chairs were produced for the expanding markets available: some of them were of attractive design and are now coming to be appreciated as cheap, pleasant and functional chairs.

216 (left) Starting with the Windsor, which goes back to the mid-18th century (see *Price Guide to Antique Furniture*) some forms of chair have been produced over very long periods. The illustration shows a typical 19th century Windsor with robust baluster turning (look at the arm supports) and a curved, or 'crinoline' stretcher. This stretcher adds more value than an ordinary, turned one. Manufacturers' catalogues show such chairs up to the 1914-18 war. Later versions tend to be less robust, however.

*1830-1920     If with yew wood, seat in elm £250 — £350*
*If in other wood £150 — £200*

217 A version of the wheelback, without the two diagonally-sloping extra spindles of 218 and 219. The turning of the legs is elegant and lacks the extra turned collars which embellish the later types and make them look more mass-produced.

*1830-1870     Arm £110 — £150*
*Single £50 — £80*

218 The 'Windsor' chair remained in use and manufacture throughout the period, as indeed it still does. Above are some straightforward mass-produced Windsors as retailed by almost every department store and furnisher.

*1860-present day     Wheelback arm £20 — £40*
*Wheelback single £15 — £20*
*Spoke-back arm £15 — £25*
*Spoke-back single £10 — £15*

219 (left and below) Windsor chairs from the Maurice Adams' catalogue of 1926, showing how the wheelback form is virtually unchanged from the previous examples from a catalogue of 1908. The wheelback 'carver' shown below, has slightly more robust baluster-turned legs but the single chair is no different from the 1908 version. The cabriole-legged wheelbacks follow an earlier 18th century design, with 'crinoline' curved stretchers. The arm chair has the curved support to the arm as against the later, turned armed support on the turned-leg chair (see No. 216).

*1920-1930*   *Cabriole-leg arm chair £80 — £120*
       *Cabriole-leg single chair £50 — £80*
       *Turned-leg arm chair £20 — £40*
       *Turned-leg single chair £15 — £20*

220 (below left and centre) Two of the most commonly-produced kitchen, country, office or institutional chairs throughout the period. On the left a single chair, usually in beech or birch with an elm or beech/birch seat. On the right, a stick-back with broad top rail, of slightly Windsor derivation.

*1860-1930*     *In sets, each £10 — £20*

221 (below right) The smoker's bow is now a popularly-hunted chair, fetching as much as £120 for certain versions in London. Good examples with opulently-turned fat baluster legs, like the one illustrated, are still to be found for much less — around £90 each — and thin, lesser versions for about £60.

*1850-1940*      *£60 — £120*
       *If in yew wood £180 — £220*

222 (left) A late 19th century chair which is a cross between a Windsor and a kitchen or office chair. It is very ornate, as the turning and the fretting of the centre splat show. There are still plenty of them about, although there has tended to be a drain of all these types of chair, particularly the Smoker's Bow, to the export trade.

*1850-1940* £70 — £95

223 (right) A typical kitchen armchair of the 19th century, on turned legs, much beloved of schools and other institutions up to the present day. Usually made in birch or beech and stained or varnished a dark colour. Sometimes the seat is made of elm. When stripped of stain or varnish to their natural colour, these chairs are often a pleasant golden brown.

*1850-1940* £35 — £55

224 Another 19th century country or kitchen chair, with a pleasantly arched and spindled decoration in the back. The seat is made of elm and the rest a pleasant, golden-coloured beech. The design was used for a long time; Shoolbred had it in 1876 and Skull in 1913.

*1850-1920* *In sets, each £25 — £40*

225 A very pretty late 19th century chair with a seat which has been recovered. Usually these chairs had an impressed plywood seat, with a pattern embossed by pressure in it, usually finished in a lighter colour than the background.

*1870-1900* *In sets, each £25 — £40*

226 A Worksop chair with robust baluster-turned legs and characteristic notched curved ends on the top rail. A fine example of this type of chair.

*c.1900* *In sets, each £50 — £70*

# CHAIRS — rocking and special purpose

227 (left) A typical turned spindled rocking chair of a type made in large numbers. This example has been re-covered.

*c.1880*          *£100 — £200*

228 A typical Edwardian child's chair in birch or beech, originally either white-painted or stained. The lower mechanism allows the chair to be set in a lower position or, additionally, to rest as a 'rocker' on the ground. Quite a common and popular child's chair in the pre-1914 period.

*1900-1914*          *£75 — £100*

229 A folding 'safari' chair, shown both open and closed, suitable for collapsing and portage by a bearer. The turned legs unscrew from the frame for further dismantling and carriage. It is made of mahogany with cane seat and back and is quite strong. When the lady concerned was tired, the chair was easily set up and she could be carried by native bearers. Made by Ward & Co. until the 1920s.

*1880-1920*          *£100 — £160*

There seems to have been a revival of the corner chair, which had languished after the end of the 18th century, in the 1870s. Why is a mystery, for it is an essentially masculine, leg-separating and inconvenient form. Richard Norman Shaw designed rush-seated corner chairs for E.W. Horsley's house Willesley, with a cabriole front leg and rather early 18th century form, stained green, in the late 1860s and, before that, a type based on late 17th century models for his own office. The corner chair fascinated Shaw, so perhaps he is responsible for its revival; his interiors show several types. It is clear from furnishers' catalogues that, by the end of the century, there was a steady demand for them.

230 Here is an early 20th century reproduction of a 'Chippendale' type, with a drop-in rush seat. The square legs and turned back supports are correct copies of the original, as are the fretted splats which are a Chippendale design. This version is made in oak to accord with the 'country' connotations of the rush seat. If made in mahogany, the drop-in seat would be upholstered. Would almost certainly be sold as 18th century.

*1900-1910*                    *£100 — £180*

231 A mahogany corner chair of much more Edwardian form but still based on 18th century design, this time late Sheraton. The drop-in seat is covered with tapestry and the back has an inlaid satinwood 'shell' in it.

*1900-1914*                    *£80 — £160*

232 (above) Another more Edwardian variant in the mahogany corner chair — the splats are of 18th century design origin but the top rail at the corner has been embellished with the pedimented shape so dear to Edwardian hearts. The seat upholstery is fixed and finished with brass studs round the edge.

*1900-1914*                    *£70 — £140*

233 A rather feebler version with a half-circular back rail and a single central splat inlaid with a Sheraton 'shell'. The thin seat and spindly legs make it look easily destructible. An intermediate step to a rounded chair — the next stage is to make the seat round instead of square.

*1900-1914*                    *£30 — £60*

234 (right) And here it is — the fully rounded 'corner' chair in which the seat as well as the back rail are of circular shape. There is now no particular reason to think of it as a corner chair except for the centrally-placed front leg, which ensures a limb-separating posture for anyone seated straight on the chair.

*1900-1914*                    *£30 — £60*

# CHAIRS — upholstered, Victorian spoon backs

The spoon back chair, usually with buttoned upholstery to the back, has become an accepted 'standard' in the antique trade following its revival in the 1960s. Many such chairs are elegant, cheerful and, as with much rococo-derived furniture, slightly frivolous in appearance. The cabriole-legged variety is the most highly valued, followed by turned-leg chairs with backs that are still in flowing curves. The later, straighter types on turned legs are not prized as highly as the early, curly ones.

**235** A good example of an open-armed Victorian button-back chair, in the rococo style, with some naturalistic carving on the front cabriole legs and the top rail of the back. An elegant, cheerful chair, fit to bring a scowl to the brow of an architect for, as Handley-Read has pointed out, the style is essentially frivolous and, therefore, not liked by architects. It was, and still is, tremendously popular. Although probably in its heyday in the 1850s and early 1860s, this style was still being made in the 1880s, as manufacturers' catalogues testify.

*1850-1885*      *£300 — £450*

**236** The 'ladies' chair' companion to the previous example. The same excellence applies: crisp carving, smart proportion, deep buttoning, flourishing cabriole legs. A classic spoon back that was popular and made throughout the period. Unfortunately, many versions were made much more cheaply and in woods much inferior to the mahogany of this example. Walnut and rosewood (rare) are in a similar quality bracket to mahogany, but beware the stained birch or beech of later examples.

*1850-1885*      *£200 — £350*

**237** Another open-armed armchair with an oval back, not buttoned in this case, although it could be. Missing its castors. Again, carved with naturalistic flora and scrolls. It can be seen that these curvaceous chairs were not for the heavier members of society: they do have a tendency to break at the joints.

*1850-1885*      *£250 — £400*

**238** (right) Another mid-Victorian chair, usually a partner to an armchair of the previous examples, with floral carving. In this case the 'waist' of the spoon is not quite as positively narrowed as one would wish — that of 236 is a better example.

*1850-1885*      *£180 — £250*

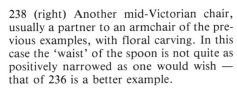

**239** A much rounder version of the spoon back with later characteristics in its rococo style — the start of cranks appearing in the flowing curves of the back. Like the other chairs, it is low and would allow the easy spread of complicated garments around it without creasing them.

*1850-1880*      *£160 — £250*

103

240 A squarer low chair which is a successor to the spoon back. It has turned legs instead of cabrioles but the back is inlaid with burr walnut or amboyna and has boxwood inlays in the top in marquetry floral forms.

*1860-1880*      *£140 — £200*

241 Square, turned-leg chairs marking the return to straighter styles prevalent from 1870 onwards. Similar to the previous example but in plain mahogany and with the characteristic dot-dash grooving (incised decoration) so typical of later semi-rococo chairs.

*1870-1890*      *Arm chair £180 — £240*
            *Single chair £120 — £160*

## CHAIRS — upholstered, Victorian uprights

As the wavy curves of the rococo died out, so a new, severer, heavier and altogether more stolid form appeared. Built rather too enduringly and associated with the graver, more portentous side of Victorian life, these chairs have not yet found great popularity and many more would have been broken up if they had not been quite so strongly built. Perhaps due for a revival.

242 This chair almost takes up where the last chairs of the previous section leave off. The back design is very similar but the arms and legs are altogether different. Note the heavy turning and the spindled gallery under the arms — very popular in the 1870s.

*1870-1890*      *£100 — £160*

243 (left) A successor to the spoon back but with classical additions, including pillars and a pedimented top. Note that the chair is missing its castors.

*1880-1890*        *£130 — £190*

244 (right) The classical and 18th century revival has arrived — note the use of the slightly Hepplewhite back, Adam-ish pillars and earlier 19th century legs but with a bit of incised grooving on the seat rail. A

...e style of 'the Louis' has intervened. ...French design of the turn of the ... which is to be found in suites of ...re for about twenty years. In a sense, ...coco is back, but in a much less ...ive form.

*...915*        *£120 — £170*

# CHAIRS — upholstered, 'designers' chairs, 1860-1910

The architects who were involved in the various design movements from 1860 onwards tended to produce chairs that were rather puritan in concept, perhaps as a reaction from the stuffed upholstery of Victorian comfort. A small selection is shown here — chairs by famous designers tend to be individually hunted and expensive.

248 (right) An oak armchair of Gothic reformed design, with all the hallmarks of the movement in its motifs, its 'revealed' construction and decoration. The use of the leather upholstery with impressed sun or sunflower motifs is also very interesting and characteristic of the interest in Japanese design at the time. The chair is a version of a popular Victorian open-arm tub chair, much found in more conventional Victorian versions.

*1860-1870*                                    *£350 — £450*

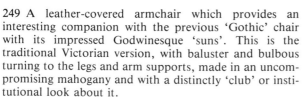

250 A chair designed by E.W. Godwin (q.v.) for the William Watt catalogue on Art Furniture of 1877. A chair subsequently much copied, particularly the back, which was admired by the Arts and Crafts Movement (q.v.).

*c.1880*      *£280 — £380*

249 A leather-covered armchair which provides an interesting companion with the previous 'Gothic' chair with its impressed Godwinesque 'suns'. This is the traditional Victorian version, with baluster and bulbous turning to the legs and arm supports, made in an uncompromising mahogany and with a distinctly 'club' or institutional look about it.

*1850-1880*                      *£250 — £350*

251 (left) This mahogany chair with tulip-pattern upholstery is of a design derived from Godwin, particularly the back, which is similar to an Anglo-Japanese type in which the uprights continue vertically well clear of the back panel. Would now be loosely called 'art nouveau' particularly due to the tulip upholstery, but it is in fact much more of an Arts and Crafts Movement chair of carefully-considered design. Note the incised ring turning on the front legs and back uprights and the way in which the arm supports sweep right down through the seat rail to the stretchers between the front and back legs.

*1885-1895*                                    *£180 — £220*

252 (right) A stained beechwood chair, also of the Arts and Crafts Movement, with twist-turned arm supports. The use of vertical straight turned spindles is rather overdone but it is, again, a very carefully thought-out design.

*c.1890*                                        *£100 — £150*

253 A more flagrantly art nouveau chair, using the flat capped uprights associated with Voysey in conjunction with inlaid 'whip-lash' floral marquetry in the rather sinuous back rail. There is a strange use of short curtain-like screens to the sides and back.

*c.1900*                        *£350 — £450*

254 A simpler and more satisfying art nouveau chair, again with flat-capped uprights and inlaid marquetry, but this time in a more solid, almost 'hall-porter's' or 'saddleback' derivation for totally enclosed comfort.

*c.1900*                        *£350 — £500*

255 The turn of the century saw an onslaught of a type of chair, neither for dining nor for long-term comfortable seating, which is aptly named 'occasional'. They were made in a variety of styles and we show a selection on these pages which cover most of the normal types. Rather than dwell individually on the stylistic origins of each chair, we are sure that our well-informed readers will derive pleasure from identifying the chairs on these three pages for themselves. The principal characteristic of most of them is their spindly nature, a surety that, were they to be used more than occasionally, they would suffer from damage.

*1900-1920*                    *£10 — £40*

## CHAIRS — upholstered, reproductions

Upholstered chairs clearly were produced to meet the demands of fashion like any other furniture. By the end of the 19th century most types of 18th century and earlier design were being produced. Some of these chairs were very well made and are now quite difficult to distinguish from the originals; others are not so successful.

256 (left) A 'French Hepplewhite' chair of high quality made in a dark mahogany. Every edge appears to be carved with gadrooning and the legs and arm supports are carved with leaves. It is very close to an 18th century chair, probably an exact copy taken from a genuine original. One can see how this design, given a little more rococo eccentricity, can become the open-armed spoon back of mid-Victorian taste.

*1880-1900*          *£300 — £400*

257 (above right) A painted armchair with caned seat and back, again in a 'Hepplewhite' design but with other 18th century connotations. Designed for drawing room use.

*1910-1920*          *£180 — £250*

258 (left) Not upholstered at all, but a good example of a 'wainscot' chair in oak emulating a mid-17th century design. The carving on the back, shaping of the arms and frieze under the seat proclaim its modernity — apart from colour and method of construction, of course.

*1900-1920*          *£90 — £140*

260 (above) An upholstered walnut arm chair in the style of the last quarter of the 17th century. Made in the 1920s and featured in Maurice Adams' book on furniture.

*c.1926*          *£80 — £120*

259 (right) A perennially popular armchair (look at any modern reproduction catalogue) in the square-legged 'Chippendale' style with curved arm supports and fully upholstered back. From a catalogue of 1910.

*1900-present day*
*Depending on condition and*
*material covering*
*£50 — £150*

261 The bergère, or caned, armchair was a popular type from about 1900 well into the 1930s and has never really died. These oak and mahogany versions are derived from similar chairs of the late 18th and early 19th century except that the oak version has been 'Jacobeanised' by the use of bobbin turning.

*1900-1930*
*Left, chair oak version £20 — £40*
*settee oak version £70 — £120*
*Right, chair mahogany version £40 — £70*
*settee mahogany version £90 — £160*

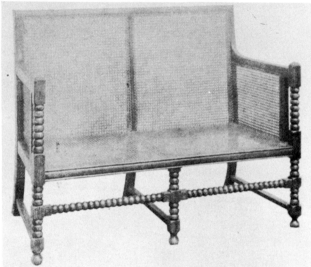

## CHAIRS — upholstered, arm and easy, 1890-1930

A mixed bag of chairs for leisure. It is not quite clear when the fully upholstered 'lounge' chair came about: probably from the 1870s onwards, when manufacturers' catalogues start to show them.

262 An armchair with inlaid decoration of the type usually associated with 'Edwardian Sheraton' furniture. The circular design of the chair is fairly typical of the Victorian period, and the front legs with their collars and fluted treatment also follow the turns that later 19th century manufacturers appear to have found irresistible.

*1880-1890*                                   *£120 — £180*

263 (right) An armchair showing again the return to 18th century designs. In this case the legs show a Sheraton influence, particularly in the stringing and cross banding of the seat rail.

*1890-1900*                                        *£100 — £160*

264 (below) Six wing easy chairs from a catalogue of c.1910.

*Depending on material and condition £40 — £180*

265 (left) Six more armchairs from the same catalogue of c.1900, showing two surprisingly '1920s' looking chairs with wooden arms and supports (bottom row left and centre) and bottom right a rocking chair.

*Top row:*
*£50 — £150*
*depending on condition*
*Bottom row,*
*left and centre:*
*£30 — £50*
*Rocking chair £45 — £65*

266 (left and right) Easy chair and settee from Maurice Adams, 1926. Out of date for some years but now coming back.

*Easy chair,*
*depending on*
*material and condition*
*£50 — £90*
*Settee, depending on*
*material and condition*
*£50 — £150*

267 (left and right) Two more easy chairs from Maurice Adams, 1926. The right-hand one is of little interest but the left-hand caned 'bergère' chair is of a type very popular in the 1930s.

*Right, depending on*
*condition and material used*
*£50 — £90*
*Left, depending on*
*condition and material used*
*£80 — £160*

The coffer endured a revival in the 1860s. After all, it is a medieval piece of furniture. The revival led to an outright spate of reproductions, rebuilds and fakes. The *Price Guide to Antique Furniture* illustrates originals and Victorian carve-ups in emulation, for it was not difficult to embellish the many plain three-band coffers which existed by adding carving to them. Some coffers must have been 'made up' by using the three-panel heads of small beds.

The antique coffer enjoyed a tremendous revival in the 1970s, spurred by the boom in antique oak and an enormous demand from the Continent. There are signs that this has now passed its zenith and a return to a more normal collecting situation, with quality and originality being appreciated, is taking place. Large numbers of Victorian reproductions, 1930s versions and outright fakes must, happily, have been exported.

## CHESTS — coffers

268 A painted chest by an enthusiast of the late 1860s or 1870s, with heavy strap hinges in wrought iron and matching wrought iron reinforcing frame on the top. The painted flowers have the appearance of sunflowers (Gothic-Anglo-Japanese-Aesthetic) and the piece follows the vogue for painted Gothic furniture associated with Burges (q.v.) who liked painted flamboyant pieces but was not too fussy about Gothic purity of motifs — he used Gothic, classical and Renaissance illustrations indiscriminately to get the flamboyant effect he liked.

*1865-1875*                               *£700 — £900*

269 (left) A 'hall coffer' by Gillows based on an adapted design of Talbert (q.v.). Reformed Gothic features include the pillars, dentillated and incised carving. The domed top is normally considered a drawback in the British Isles because the piece cannot then be used for a table or seat.

*1870-1880*                               *£400 — £500*

270 (right) From original interpretations to an out-and-out reproduction of high quality. It is possible that this was a plain, three-panel oak coffer of correct period, to which carved and inlaid decoration has been added. There is an honest look about the feet, formed by carrying down the joined frame, but the carved decoration and inlays give rise to doubts. Certainly, the arcaded panels (used often enough in 'correct' coffers) have a new, crisp look about them and the decoration inlaid into the three panels does not ring true to period.

*1890-1920*                *£450 — £600*

271 An oak chest or coffer which copies a 17th and 18th century piece of furniture. The front is embellished with three panels featuring vertical ribbed treatment in imitation of linenfold carving. The legs, which are a continuation of the end frame — true to tradition — are a little thin for a period piece and perhaps a little high, lacking wear at the foot. Intended in 1900-1915 as a hall piece for storage of travelling rugs.

*1900-1916*                                    *£100 — £120*

272 (right and top right) Simple six-plank oak coffers from Maurice Adams' book of 1926. Reasonably true to the original type.

*c.1925*                                    *£60 — £120*

273 A three-panel simple oak coffer of the 1920s. The proportion is a bit too elongated vertically to be mistaken for an original piece.

*c.1925*                                    *£100 — £180*

274 A mule chest of the 1920s in plain oak. The two drawers below are fielded and the shaped fielded panels to the front are taken from 17th century forms. Now used at the end of the bed — to put the quilt in.

*c.1925*                                    *£100 — £180*

116

# CHESTS OF DRAWERS — 1860-1930

The period 1860-1930 is not particularly associated with beautiful chests of drawers in the traditional antique collector's view. Wooden knobs and nasty turned feet are what spring immediately to mind. Unlike the 18th century, where the chest played a decorative role, the chest of drawers was relegated to the bedroom in the 19th century and replaced by display cabinets and other pieces in the more public rooms. Thus the pieces tend to be commodious and very functional, with some design aberrations as a gesture to current taste, but not very lovely.

At the end of the century, back went the chest to 18th century styling in addition to current forms. It was perhaps the Arts and Crafts Movement who reclaimed the chest of drawers as a more interesting piece and, subsequently, the Cotswold designers — Gimson, the Barnsleys and Gordon Russell — produced pieces in solid native woods that were based on traditional forms but clean in line and of pleasing appearance. The trade always produced pine and deal chests in quantity and the chest also appeared, of course, in Jacobethan, burr walnut bedappled and plain forms.

275 (right) A mahogany chest of drawers with twist-turned columns down the sides and a heavy, serpentine-moulded top drawer. The mahogany veneers used are of high quality, with well-matched figure repeated from drawer to drawer, but the overall effect is heavy. It is a type popular from the 1840s onwards, although by 1880 it must have been out of fashion.

*1840-1870*                                    *£120 — £150*

276 Another chest in mahogany of sub-classical design of a type originating in the 1840s and based on French classical types. Well made, with well matched veneers but nowadays considered ponderous.

*1840-1860*                    *£150 — £200*

277 A mahogany chest with three deep drawers at the top. Sometimes the middle deep top drawer is fitted as a secretaire, which adds to value. The quality of veneers is good but the effect is ponderous, particularly the bottom apron which appears to have a drawer in it. These chests, like the previous two, were built usually of deal, with mahogany veneer, for cheapness and many now suffer from missing pieces of veneer due to wear. It is not difficult to repair small missing pieces but the effect before repair tends to put purchasers off.

*1850-1870*                                    *£80 — £120*

278 (left) Another ponderous chest, but this time bow-fronted. Not really of the correct proportions for modification to an '18th century' bow front on splayed feet by a 'converter', so has to be sold more or less for what it is.

*1850-1880*                            *£80 — £120*

279 (right) Possibly the epitome of the good quality Victorian mahogany chest of drawers — tall, bow fronted, with splendid use of 'feather' mahogany veneers. Capacious, well-built and with drawers fitted to run smoothly. The wooden knobs have been turned with some decorative ridging which refines the bluntness of the ordinary bulbous knob. The bun-shaped and tapered turned feet are also typical. The gradation of the drawer depths is also well handled on this example. Altogether a very professional piece of furniture but, unlike 18th century chests, not very suitable for rooms other than the bedroom and therefore restricted in price accordingly.

*1850-1870*                            *£90 — £140*

280 (left) A chest made by Shoolbred & Co. in emulation of a French Empire style, with a marble top. It is made in solid mahogany with mahogany veneered drawer fronts and solid mahogany mouldings, so must have been expensive. Now considered somewhat dark and sombre, so not particularly valued.

*1870-1885*                            *£100 — £160*

281 (right) Back to the 18th century — a mahogany bow-fronted chest on splay feet in the 'Hepplewhite' style but with original wooden knobs, whereas Hepplewhite would have had pressed brass plates and handles. Made in quite large quantities and now often 'converted' to an 18th century piece by modification back to brass handles. If a bit tall for 18th century proportion, then it might be further modified by having a drawer removed and the carcase re-jigged.

*1880-1900*                            *£180 — £220*

282 (left) A 'Chippendale' mahogany serpentine fronted chest of drawers, with a brushing slide and canted corners with blind fretted decoration, on bracket feet. A good reproduction of a mid-18th century chest.

*1900-1910*
*£150 — £250*

283 (right) A mahogany serpentine-fronted chest on chest incorporating two short drawers, six long drawers and a brushing slide. The canted corners are embellished with blind fretwork of Chippendale pattern and the top moulding is dentilled. Although the quality of workmanship appears to be good, the proportion is too cramped for 18th century work. Doubtless a useful piece for the smaller rooms of the early 20th century.

*1910-1930*                                                    *£300 — £450*

284 (right) An Edwardian mahogany chest of drawers, on a solid plinth base, with satinwood crossbanding and oval pressed brass handles to give a 'Sheraton' look.

*1900-1910*                                                    *£50 — £90*

285 (left) A typical Edwardian chest of drawers, with solid plinth base. Available at the time in either 'satin walnut' — which is a kind of solid yellow-brown wood, imported from America — or oak. It has pressed bronze handles and plates. The incised horizontal moulding machined across the drawer fronts and down the sides is a feature of the period.

*1900-1910*                                                    *£60 — £80*

119

286 Another typical Edwardian form of chest, known at the time as a 'Scotch' chest. The drawer edges are bevelled or fielded. The arrangement of the top drawers, with one deep central unit and pairs of small drawers flanking it, dates back to press chests of the 18th century. Available in walnut or mahogany.

*1900-1910*        *£70 — £100*

287 An oak chest of drawers of slightly progressive design with 'oxidised' metal handles. A reduction by a commercial manufacturer of 'art nouveau' styling to a simpler form — Plain Furniture is on the way.

*1900-1910*        *£30 — £45*

288 (right) A cupboard chest of drawers favoured by Percy Wells for use in the bedroom, where the fall-front cupboard, intended for hats, had 'met with cordial approval'. Presumably this was intended for ladies, since the vision of lustful 1920s male cottage visitors, dashing into the bedroom with their hats still on, having missed the hall stand or rack recommended by Wells (elsewhere) in their ardour on the way, and stuffing the offending garment into the top of the cupboard chest (before or afterwards?) 'with cordial approval' is even more than D.H. Lawrence might conceive. Actually Wells also recommended similar cupboard chests, with added boot and book shelves below and above respectively, for the living room. There is a hint that the fall front chest might replace the bureau, using the flap for writing purposes.

c.1920        £20 — £40

289 Three waxed oak chests by Maurice Adams, showing reliance on late 17th and early 18th century designs. A turned-leg stretchered variety for the raised first example, called a 'Cromwell' design by the maker; bracket feet and bun feet for the more conventional types.

*c.1925*      *'Cromwell' £30 — £45*
*Conventional chests £50 — £80*

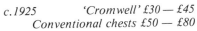

290 Three mahogany reproduction style chests from Maurice Adams. The feet are a semi-cabriole splayed variety in deference to prevailing 'good' taste, i.e. for quasi-Queen Anne.

*c.1925*      *£50 — £90*

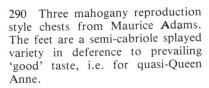

291 Chest of drawers in oak with walnut handles by Gordon Russell. Wardrobe and mirror to match. Note the inlaid ebony-and-box chequer lines beloved of the movement, particularly the Cotswold Crafties. Simple and functional: the wooden handles are a particular trademark of Russell's.

*c.1930*                         *Chest £300 — £400*

## CHESTS — dressing

The dressing chest appears to be a Victorian invention and, although out of favour for some years, it was quite a good idea. The addition of a mirror to a normal chest of drawers was a quite common form but sometimes the chest top was modified into a minor dressing table top with small drawers and cubby holes. A lot of such chests have had the mirrors removed to convert them into ordinary chests of drawers, but the pine dressing chest appears to be less subject to such modification.

292 (below) A bamboo and rattan dressing chest with a small drawer under the mirror and three long drawers below. Decorative and now quite fashionable.

*1890-1900*                         *£130 — £180*

293 Two pine dressing chests with characteristic, shaped cresting rails to the mirrors, also shown under Pine Furniture, as 382.

*1890-1920*                         *£80 — £130*

294 (left) An Edwardian pedimented dressing chest, available in a stained oak or mahogany colour, with the characteristic broken pediment to the top rail of the mirror. The top of the chest has been fitted with two small drawers under a shelf.

*1900-1920* *£50 — £85*

295 (right) An oak dressing chest known as a 'combination' chest due to the tiled splashback to the washstand section, the swing mirror and the cupboard, with a towel rail to the side. A combination of washstand and dressing chest or table with incised grooving across the drawers.

*1900-1920* *£35 — £55*

296 Another 'combination' chest, this time white enamelled, with tiled splashback and towel rail. Note the shaped cresting rails above mirror and splashback.

*1900-1920* *£40 — £65*

297 (left) A white enamelled chest with mirror between turned uprights. Many such chests have had the mirror removed and been treated to the pine stripper's caustic tank.

*1900-1920* *£40 — £70*

298 (right) A dressing chest from Percy Wells' book on furniture for small houses of 1920. The form is simplified but stiffer and rather Spartan. Utilitarian, yes; cheerful, no.

*c.1920* *£20 — £40*

299 (right) A mahogany military chest fitted with a secretaire drawer. This secretaire arrangement can be extended for the whole drawer length or confined to a smaller central section as shown here.

*1845-1865*                    *£600 — £900*

300 A military chest on turned feet. These chests were used by army officers up to the 1870s. The flush-fitting drawer handles and brass-reinforced corners are their characteristic features, as are the carrying handles to each half. Usually made in mahogany, but padouk, cedar and camphorwood examples are found. Now much reproduced in a variety of woods, including 'distressed' yew veneers and available in large quantities in reproduced form. There is not a lot of difference in price between reproductions and 19th century examples.

*1800-1870*                    *£400 — £600*

301 (right) A camphorwood military secretaire chest of Anglo-Indian origin. This example is slightly more ornate than usual, since it includes a wooden gallery rail around the top which incorporates scrolled carving for decoration. The style of the carving derives from rococo ornamentation of earlier Victorian popularity. The central secretaire section contains a fitted interior. The brass reinforcing plates at the joints and the flush handles are characteristic and the turned feet are removable. A high quality version in a desirable wood.

*c.1860*                    *£1,300 — £1,700*

# CHESTS — Wellington and specimen

Wellington chests should more correctly be called specimen chests, since that is what they are for. Why the Great Duke's name has been used for them is not clear; he was an inventive man, although he disliked inventors, but there does not seem to be any record of his hand in their design. The lockable flaps, which hold the drawers in place, might make the piece a useful campaign item but when Loudon illustrated a similar chest in 1833 the Duke had not campaigned for nearly twenty years. The type was long-lived, being illustrated by Smee (1850), Shoolbred (1876) and Light (1881).

302 (right) A rather plain Wellington chest of sub-classical Loudon-like design made in mahogany. The third and fourth 'drawers' down are in fact false; the fronts are *trompe-l'œil* on a single flap which lowers for a writing surface, revealing secretaire fittings inside.

*1830-1860*                                           *£300 — £450*

303 (left) A Wellington chest in feathered satinwood with ebony stringing lines. There is a brass gallery rail around the top. Furniture in woods with 'satin' finishes is often associated with Holland & Sons who produced items in this style in the 1850s and 1860s.

*1850-1870*                                           *£450 — £600*

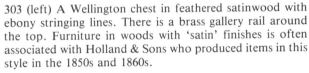

304 A figured walnut secretaire Wellington chest with the usual turned wooden drawer knobs. Again there is a sub-classical scroll at the top of the locking side flaps like that used on 302. Similarly, the third and fourth drawers conceal a secretaire section and are on a false front which lowers to act as a writing surface. The wood surfaces are more decorative and lighter in tone — hence the higher price.

*1850-1880*                *£400 — £500*

305 A carved oak 'Wellington' chest with lion-mask carved handles to the drawers. A version of the popular form of Wellington or specimen chest which meets the vogue for carved oak furniture of medieval appearance which started in the 1880s.

*1880-1910*                *£350 — £500*

306 Not really anything to do with Wellington chests, but a 20th century specimen chest-on-chest made of oak with wooden drawer knobs having carefully-faceted front surfaces. Very much designed in the manner of Gimson or one of the Arts and Crafts—Cotswold school of the first quarter of the 20th century.

*1900-1925*                *£200 — £350*
*If attributable to, say, Gimson £700 — £1,000*

# DESKS — davenports

The davenport desk has been associated with the Victorian period for so long that it seems strange to conjecture that its popularity was possibly in decline by the 1880s. The name comes from Gillow's Cost Books of the 1790s — 'Captain Davenport, a desk' written alongside the design. So the davenport was initially a Georgian and, later, a Regency piece of furniture, before the Victorians took it up. The earliest forms are, as expected, squarer, and it was the 1850s that brought about the rococo scrolled, cabriole leg form of front support in place of the pillars that arose in the 1820s and 1830s. Readers of the *Price Guide to Antique Furniture* will have followed the development of these earlier types.

By 1860 the scrolled supports were slowly disappearing in favour of pillars of debased classical form and, finally, were dropped altogether. There is overlap in all these designs, as the catalogues of Smee, Booth, Shoolbred and Light show. There were even Reformed Gothic davenports from Richard Charles in 1866. But the period 1860-1890 in general saw a rather stiffer form of davenport, as though the rococo curves of the 1850s had been straightened up in favour of something that did not go back to Georgian severity and cleanliness of line, but which met the demand for a more Louis XVI look and, finally, the vogue for ebonised and spindly-turned ornamentation. Heal's catalogue of 1884 shows several rather mean examples, not cheap for their time, but stiff, with predictably machined turning or bas relief carving. Not many ebonised examples seem to have survived and by the early 20th century other forms of small desk seem to have supplanted the davenport.

The thing to look for in Davenports is burr walnut — nowadays by far the most popular type of this period — followed by rosewood, walnut, and, far behind, mahogany. Ebonised davenports are an acquired taste.

307 (above) A high quality burr walnut 'harlequin' davenport with a 'piano' shaped top with a lid that lifts to reveal a pull-out writing slide. The superstructure has a hinged letter rack operating on a spring mechanism released by a button inside a short drawer. The piece has inlaid boxwood stringing and stylised flowers. The drawers down the side in view are genuine sliding drawers, whilst on the other side there are four dummy drawer fronts. This is the normal, and preferred arrangement except for examples where the drawers are contained inside a cupboard door. An example which has all the high-quality features and gadgetry associated with the highly-prized versions. A very similar model is illustrated in Shoolbred, 1876.

*1860-1880*                                   *£900 — £1,100*

308 (right) An interesting form of burr-walnut davenport of a design shown in catalogues of the 1870s and 1880s but which owes something to the 1860s in its use of veneers and naturalistic fretted carving. The two top upper doors open to reveal letter compartments and, in some versions, small drawers. There is a frieze drawer which contains a hinged writing slope. A side door in the lower section, panelled with a carved fretted adornment, opens to reveal four drawers. The piece is inlaid with boxwood stringing and stylised flowers. Not as expensive a form as the piano top but still a highly-prized piece.

*1860-1880*          *£850 — £1,000*

309 (above) A rosewood davenport of the cabriole leg type of front support, using the scrolling rococo form popular in the 1850s. A design which was still made for another twenty years, though it must have been thoroughly out of fashion by the 1880s. The fretted top gallery shows an alternative form to the lidded stationery compartment of protruding type shown in the other examples.

*1850-1880*          *£500 — £650*

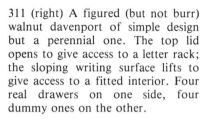

310 (left) An interesting and unusual oak davenport in Gothic style with clustered column supports. Gothic style davenports were illustrated by Pugin himself in 1835 — but a much more Regency, elaborate 'Gothick' form — and in the Reformed Gothic manner by Richard Charles in 1866 and C. & R. Light in 1881. The style of this davenport is more of the earlier Victorian unreformed variety but could have been repeated by later makers.

*1850-1860*          *£600 — £850*

311 (right) A figured (but not burr) walnut davenport of simple design but a perennial one. The top lid opens to give access to a letter rack; the sloping writing surface lifts to give access to a fitted interior. Four real drawers on one side, four dummy ones on the other.

*1870-1890*          *£350 — £500*

314 (below) The end of the line for davenports from a catalogue of c.1910. No pillars, an inlaid 'Sheraton' satinwood banding and no decoration to speak of on the cheap stained mahogany, doubtless finished with French polish.

*c.1910*          *£200 — £350*

312 (above) An Aesthetic Movement ebonised davenport with characteristic design features — painted panels, this time of birds, panelled construction and rather fussy turning. At the top of the pillars there is a curious Anglo-Japanese bracket just to show that the makers had kept up with Godwin and the latest taste.

*c.1880*          *£450 — £650*

313 A really late Victorian form in mahogany with little pretension to elegance and very stiff in execution. The turned columns have lost their way and are not sure what form to take. The base is plain and rigid. A panel has been suggested by applied mouldings. The top retains the features of the earlier davenports, however, and the inherent usefulness of the type.

*1885-1900*          *£300 — £450*

The Victorian era was a great boom time for the pedestal desk, which was clearly much more popular for a long time than the fall-front or cylinder bureau. Not only for domestic use but also for equipping the thousands of offices which developed throughout the industrial scene, this form was adaptable to several varieties and types of wood. On the whole, oak and mahogany prevailed due to their endurance. Walnut and other woods, apart from pine, tend to be more highly valued for this reason.

The desk was made and reproduced throughout the entire period covered by this book (and still is). Where possible, approximate dates have been shown but some types such as 'Georgian partners' or 'Chippendale' can be very difficult to date precisely.

315 A handsome burr walnut pedestal desk with superstructure including a sloping writing surface, drawers and a turned baluster gallery. A type of desk once rather despised for its superstructure, which was often removed to convert the piece into a flat-topped pedestal desk of more Georgian appearance. Now, however, the form is coming into its own as a genuine Victorian one with its own usefulness.

*1855-1885*               *£650 — £900*

316 (right) A mahogany cylinder bureau with a kneehole. The pedestals each have three drawers and under the sliding tambour there is a writing surface with six small drawers and letter compartments. It is a type illustrated in several catalogues of the 1870s and 1880s, although the design goes back to earlier George III forms. This is a very plain version.

*1870-1890*               *£450 — £600*

317 (left) A highly decorated Reformed Gothic desk in a style which brings Burges, Seddon, Talbert and Eastlake to mind. Burges and Seddon would go for such lavish decoration; all of them would use the diagonal planking and pillared columns with central collars. It is interesting to compare this version of Gothic with that of 'Chippendale' shown in no. 325 in this section.

*1860-1870*               *£2,000 — £4,000*

318 (right) The designer of this pedestal desk has imbibed more than a little of the spirit of Reformed Gothic — note the panelled sides and slightly 'revealed' construction, with shaped feet.

*c.1880*            *£1,500 — £2,500*

319 (below) A mahogany pedestal desk of a type made fairly continuously throughout Victoria's reign and onwards to the present day. There is a tooled leather top, three drawers in the frieze and three drawers in each pedestal. The moulded edge is a fairly bold type and so is the thumb nail moulding around the base.

*1860-1890*            *£350 — £500*

320 A plain mahogany pedestal partners' desk of large dimensions — three feet by six feet — with drawers in each opposing side, the concept being that the two partners involved could work at the same desk, facing each other.

*1870-1890 but a type made on into the present day*
*£1,000 — £2,000*

321 A carved oak pedestal desk with characteristic lion-mask carved handles to the drawers. The late Victorians and Edwardians were fond of carved oak — a taste for the medieval transmitted to them by the work of the Gothic reformers, who would have hated this piece.

*1895-1915*            *£400 — £600*

322 A further version of a carved oak pedestal desk with lion-mask carved handles. The 'Elizabethan' effect has been taken a stage further by the inclusion of reeded bulbs on the legs. More carving has been packed on in foliage form and the top edge is also carved with leaf forms.

*c.1900*            *£650 — £1,000*

323 (left) A mahogany cylinder bureau or pedestal desk on serpentine feet with a pierced brass gallery rail around the top. The piece is inlaid with marquetry of 18th century inspiration (Adam, Hepplewhite and Sheraton all spring to mind) including the splendid central vase in an oval panel on the cylinder front and swags, husks, leaf and floral decoration elsewhere. It has been said of other 'Edwardian Sheraton' pieces that the craftsmen of this period had a tendency to over-egg the pudding and this piece is inclined towards an example of this trait. There is just a bit too much decoration, a tendency to flashiness which distinguishes the piece from its 18th century original. A handsome piece, nevertheless, requiring some first class craftmanship to execute.

*1890-1910*                                    *£1,400 — £2,000*

324 (right) A mahogany partners' pedestal desk on carved serpentine bracket feet in 'Chippendale' style. The canted corners are carved with leaf and foliage decoration and the top edge is gadrooned. The top is inset with tooled leather. A straightforward high quality piece which states that it is reproduction from the carved decoration.

*1910-1930*                    *£1,000 — £2,000*

325 A mahogany pedestal desk in the early Georgian manner, with clustered columns on the pedestal corners and Gothic blind fret tracery around the frieze. There are three drawers in the frieze on the viewed side, with three drawers in each pedestal below. The out-of-view side has three drawers in the frieze and cupboards below — an arrangement normally fitted to a 'partners' desk but in fact allowing the desk to be viewed favourably from both sides. The quality of workmanship and carving is high — note the carved moulded edge to the top and the plinth around the base.

*1920-1940*                    *£1,500 — £2,500*

326 A walnut 'Queen Anne' kneehole desk, made as an accurate reproduction of a period piece. The top is quarter veneered and the drawers have a diagonal banding and lip moulding round the edges. The pierced handles are a little late in design for the period of the desk, but otherwise the proportions and restraint of the veneers are a good copy.

*1920-1930*                    *£350 — £500*

327 (right) A somewhat 1930s interpretation in the use of matched figures walnut veneers on the drawer fronts but without excessive over-figure or burring ('Queen Anne' versions of pedestal desks, with feather banding, etc., etc., were not uncommon in the 1930s). The choice of ring handles, however, if original, is odd.

*1920-1930*                    *£800 — £1,400*

328 (left) An inlaid mahogany kidney-shaped pedestal desk or writing table in the Sheraton manner, with boxwood inlaid stringing lines and set on square tapering legs ending in brass castors. The top is inset with tooled leather. The kidney-shaped desk is a perennial favourite and can often be highly decorative, with burr veneers and marquetry adding enormously to value

*1890-1930*                    *£600 — £850*

329 (right) A rather spindly cabriole-legged writing table-cum-pedestal desk, half way between either definition, which shows how, in Edwardian times, there was a movement towards versions of the 'Queen Anne' style which heralded the outburst of burrs and cabrioles of the 1920s. In this case the decoration of the drawers is late 18th/early 19th century Sheraton in origin, whereas the legs are somewhat apologetic cabrioles, i.e. a version of an early 18th century style. The piece is in mahogany, which is not a Queen Anne wood.

*1900-1910*                    *£250 — £350*

330 (left) A high quality mahogany pedestal desk, on square tapering legs, with inlaid boxwood stringing lines. There is a brass gallery rail about four inches high at the back, which has a diamond-pattern fret. By using the stringing lines to describe panels on the drawer fronts and facings of the frame, the makers have managed to convey the impression of a restrained, quality piece.

*c.1900*                    *£500 — £900*

331 (right) A mahogany half-pedestal desk of Sheraton style with drawers banded in satinwood. The top is inset with tooled leather.

*1900-1910*
*£90 — £180*

332 (left) Figured walnut and cabriole legs — a 1920s pedestal desk of considerable quality, showing the onset of the modified Queen Anne styles which became so popular. This is a slightly more modernised approach than the slavish copies of the style that were prevalent.

*1920-1930*
*£400 — £800*

## DESKS — roll-top

333 (right) A rather fine oak roll-top desk in which something of Eastlake's preaching on Gothic reformed furniture has taken effect. Note the panelled sides, the incised line decoration on the drawers and the carved trefoil motif on the slope frame. Undoubtedly intended for use by some professional of 'reformed' leanings.

*c.1875*                                          *£1,400 — £2,200*

334 (left) An oak roll-top pedestal desk with panelled sides shown open to reveal a generously complex fit-up of pigeon holes, small drawers and letter racks inside. There are four drawers in each pedestal and a pull-out shelf at either side.

*1900-1920*                                          *£550 — £700*

335 An oak roll-top desk similar to the previous example but with a simpler inside fit-up, no foot rail and not panelled at the back.

*1900-1920*                    *£400 — £600*

336 An oak roll-top desk with a wooden top gallery intended as a bookshelf and fitted with metal drawer handles. The inside has a relatively simple fit-up of two drawers, pigeon holes and ink wells. There is a foot rail and the back is panelled. The piece is on castors.

*1900-1920*                    *£300 — £500*

337 A half-pedestal oak roll-top desk with metal drawer handles based on the previous model in design.

*1900-1920*                    *£100 — £200*

338 An oak roll-top desk with ring handles to the drawers. It has a solid frieze around the bottom but is mounted on castors. Quite a complex fit-up to the interior but not as desirable as the example shown in No. 334.

*1900-1920*                    *£300 — £500*

# DESKS — Wootton Patent Office (Wells Fargo)

This form has become a category almost to itself, with a ready market in the USA, from which it originates. Usually made in American walnut with figured panels in more desirable versions, but also found in mahogany. The genre originates from around 1870 and appears in a variety of designs of single- or double-opening types with more or less complicated interiors. Really complex large decorative versions are highly sought after and price is affected accordingly. Often referred to, loosely, as a 'Wells Fargo' desk by those fond of watching TV.

339 A good quality walnut Wootton Patent Office desk of the double-doored type, shown closed. Note the fielded panels with ebonised moulding, the figured woods and the highly-carved top shelf. There are letter boxes fitted in the doors so that correspondence can be delivered to the owner while he is away and the piece is locked up.

*c.1870*                      *£1,500 — £2,200*

340 Another Wootton desk, this time shown with the doors open to illustrate the quantity and variety of pigeon holes and drawers in the piece. The writing surface, which conceals more fitments, is shown in the 'up' position, i.e. closed. The top is not carved like the previous example and the wood is mahogany.

*c.1880*         *£1,200 — £2,000*

341 Another Wootton desk, this time of the single-opening door type, but with panels and drawers veneered with decorative burr walnut. Although the single-door is not always as convenient as the double-door and tends to off-balance the piece, this version has a complex and attractive interior.

*c.1880* *£900 — £1,500*

342 A large double-door version with elaborate interior and carved top similar to 339, shown closed. A handsome piece.

*c.1880* *£1,500 — £2,200*

# DRESSERS

The term 'dresser' comes from the side table used for the 'dressing' of food in the medieval hall. The form which was used in kitchens of the 17th and 18th centuries was still unchanged in the early 19th. Indeed kitchen furniture, as a general rule, has been the least subject to the vagaries of fashion. The dressers illustrated here show how the piece seems to have become acceptable as a piece of furniture which could be used either in the kitchen or the dining room of the cottage or modest house. Mainly the styles reflect the popular taste for oak furniture of Stuart or Jacobean type but modern versions, in art nouveau or Edwardian styles were also made. The simplest type of dresser, illustrated by Percy Wells in the 1920s, shows little change from its predecessor of a hundred years before; it is an enduringly useful form.

Due to the tremendous rise in popularity and price of antique dressers, the late Victorian version has now also become expensive as these examples show. Pine dressers of more modest price have also become very fashionable and the fact that a pine dresser may be virtually brand new does not seem affect price very much provided it is an attractive version.

343 (left) An oak sideboard of commercial manufacture which comes quite close to the spirit of the original period from which it derives. It seems that the designers of such pieces were always surer in their touch with the top halves. It is the cabriole front legs which disappoint; they are too curvaceous, too wavy to provide the 'Queen Anne' solidity and proportion that one seeks. The three deep drawers could have done with a fielded effect also, to relate them to the top.

*1900-1920*                                                    *£300 — £450*

344 (below) An oak dresser in a style which derives from court cupboards of the early 17th century and later influences. The top half in its way is impressive, even if the downward-going turned knobs do conflict with the upward-going turned pillars with their bulbous bases. The lower half is less sure, as the turned legs are thinner and the stretcher arrangement an eyesore. Inconsistency has triumphed by putting applied split balusters on the end stiles but a split bobbin turning at the centre. The asymmetric arrangement of a cupboard with two doors occupying one side and two drawers the other is purely 20th century.

*1900-1920*                                                    *£300 — £400*

345 An oak dresser in the 'William and Mary' style, incorporating a central top cupboard with an Hollandish arch and fielded door panel. The base has inverted-cup turning to the legs and a pot-board stretcher. The shaping of the friezes is consistent with the style, but the flat-capped top moulding is typically Edwardian.

*1900-1910*                                    *£300 — £400*

346 An oak 'Jacobean' dresser with much twist turning to the legs, stretchers and tier shelf supports. The central and top aprons are shaped with stylistically consistent forms, but the two side cupboards, while doubtless useful, are borrowed from the 18th century sideboard. Geometric applied mouldings to drawer and cupboard doors complete the Jacobean effect. A bold and decorative piece.

*1910-1920*                                    *£300 — £400*

347 Another oak 'Jacobean' dresser sporting art nouveau handles to the drawers which are set beside a pair of cupboard doors in an asymmetric arrangement. Twist turned legs, stretchers and top supports and a rather more expensively panelled back than the usual vertical planking.

*1910-1920*                                    *£200 — £350*

348 (left) Although in oak, this dresser exhibits the typical bas-relief machined carving in panels, also to be found on walnut and mahogany furniture of this period. The weakest point of the design is the use of the prissy cabriole front legs and scrolled bottom apron. If these are ignored, the base and top half are quite a bold, well-proportioned construction.

*1900-1920*
*£300 — £400*

349 An oak dresser with twist-turned front legs and inlaid boxwood and ebony stringing lines to the panels on the very deep drawers. Borrowing a bit from the Jacobean in design and a bit from the Arts and Crafts Movement.

*1900-1920*                                    *£250 — £350*

350 (above left) An open oak dresser by the same maker as the previous example, 349, but without the smashable glazed centre door disapproved of by Percy Wells (see 353). The use of ebony and boxwood diagonally-banded stringing lines and inlays seems to have originated with Arts and Crafts Movement designers and remained popular in the 1910-1925 period.

*1910-1925*                                              *£200 — £300*

351 (above right) An oak dresser on 'Queen Anne' cabriole front legs and plain construction but with a centre cupboard to the top shelf with a glazed door showing a stained glass tulip motif as decoration. Quite an Arts and Crafts addition to a commercial mass-produced piece.

*1900-1920*                                              *£150 — £200*

352 (right) An oak dresser of plain construction sporting a set of art nouveau hinges to the doors, otherwise unremarkable.

*1900-1920*                                              *£90 — £120*

353 (right) A dresser from Percy Wells c.1920, intended to be made from whitewood and stained light brown. It is 3ft.6ins. wide and the top is "not to high to dust". Wells was concerned with designs for new cottages in which there would be a kitchen-living room combined, in which such a dresser would stand. He was worried about the use of glass doors in the upper part, as recommended by the 'Women's Housing Sub-Committee' (shades of 1984) because glass doors would add to cost. Since the china on the shelves would be used three times a day, there would be little time for it "to get dusty". Glass doors would mean "more work to keep them clean" and "expense if the glass got broken". (Presumably this would happen when the husband of the wife emancipated from dusting and cleaning meretricious ornaments, hurled his beer mug at his spouse.) Wells preferred solid doors instead of glass. The dresser was intended to be in the living room, thus preventing the purchase of a modern, cheap chiffonier or sideboard — "anything but good or pleasant". The rails of the doors are chamfered on the inside edges, but a plain rounded surface "is better than a chamfer" as far as "leaving no edge at all for dust to settle on". Banter apart, the piece is useful, functional and proportionally well designed. A desirable unit which is virtually ageless unless the built-in kitchen takes over completely — including the dining room.

*c.1920*                                          *£150 — £250*

354 (below right) A small dresser of Percy Wells design, c.1920, apparently in oak but also conceived for whitewood, stained a light brown, waxed and set with a rubber polish. The shelf at the back was intended for china or books. The terms 'dresser' and 'sideboard' were somewhat interchangeable to Wells, who visualised the use of such a piece in either the kitchen or living room — rooms which were combined into one large room in contemporary designs for new cottages. He was quite right to say that it is difficult to see where a dresser ends and a sideboard begins, but took a tier of shelves as being the definitive feature of a dresser.

*c.1920*                                          *£70 — £140*

355 (left) A dwarf dresser from Wells, c.1920, of simple and straightforward design. Almost down to a kitchen cupboard but still conceived from Wells' dresser principle — certainly low enough to dust. It is interesting to compare this unit with the one designed by Ambrose Heal — see p. 34.

*c.1920*              *£40 — £75*

356 A walnut dresser base on cabriole legs connected by moulded stretchers. The three drawers are veneered in burr walnut and have a herringbone inlay between the burr veneer and the crossbanding. The piece is an interesting interpretation of a 'Queen Anne' style, with rather high-quality cabrioles ending in a squared hoof-type foot and with shell motifs carved on the knees. There is a solid half-round moulding applied to the carcase edge around the drawers. The stretchers are an agreeable fantasy, quite unnecessary structurally and of a form derived from the cross-stretchers of the William and Mary period. Not knowing quite how to use the cross-stretcher idea between an uneven number of legs — five — the maker has compromised by putting in straight ones around the sides and back, and then has connected his traditional ogee curves to the back one by means of a semi-circular one in each case.

*1920-1940*                                                                                        *£90 — £180*

357 An oak dresser base from Maurice Adams, the stout column-turned baluster front legs of which are let down badly by the weak stretchers and back legs. There are two cupboard doors and two deep drawers with applied geometric mouldings in the Jacobean manner.

*1920-1930*                         *£140 — £200*

The Victorians were rather fond of somewhat florid mirrors and overmantels, mostly made by building up gesso or plaster on a wood frame and subsequently gilding the surface. Some carved wood mirrors were made as well and these are, obviously, the most expensive type. Overmantels of the very large type are now difficult to place and require large walls with high ceilings, but the oval and circular wall mirrors, or girandoles, are being re-appreciated now that it is possible to touch up the faded or discoloured gilding with one of the many proprietary types of gold waxes and paints available for the purpose.

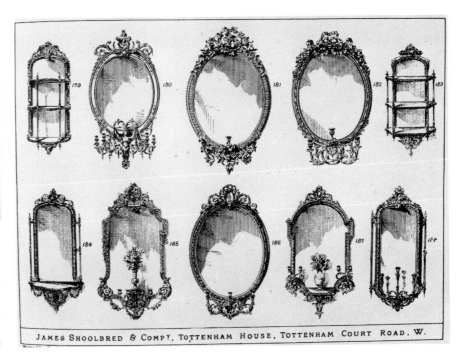

JAMES SHOOLBRED & COMPY. TOTTENHAM HOUSE, TOTTENHAM COURT ROAD, W.

358 'Girandoles' from Shoolbred's catalogue of 1876. The decoration is made of plaster, subsequently treated with gesso and gilded. Until comparatively recently these ornate pieces were considered somewhat vulgar but prices have been mounting steadily in the last few years.

*1876*                    *£150 — £350*

360 An oval gilt mirror of the gesso and plaster type with 18th century rococo styling. Mirrors of this type appear to have been popular in the later 19th century, when many reproductions of 18th century types were featured in furnishers' catalogues.

*1870-1890*        *£180 — £250*

359 A small Victorian gilt circular mirror or girandole of a type illustrated by Shoolbred and other furnishers in catalogues of the 1870s and 1880s. Based on rococo designs and 'naturalistic' motifs. Made of plaster on a wooden frame and about two feet (60 cm) in diameter.

*1870-1880*                    *£80 — £120*

361 A really ornate rococo mirror with great depth to the frame which is surmounted by a cherub figure of Cupid, holding a bow. The depth is remarkable and the shape of the oval mirror is elegant.

*1900-1920    Carved wood £1,000 — £1,500*
*Gesso £400 — £650*

141

363 (right) A carved rococo mirror, with scroll and leaf forms, which is again an imitation of an eighteenth century style.

*Early 20th century*
*£150 — £250*

362 A rococo oval wall mirror in emulation of mid-18th century carved mirrors incorporating similar birds and decoration. Made of giltwood and plaster. Very decorative and of good quality.

*1900-1925*                    *£300 — £450*

364 An oval gilded mirror of 'Empire' design with seated griffins on either side of a classical urn with Olympic torch as a decorative cresting. The solid frame to the bevelled mirror has gilded edges and gilded classical motifs on a painted background.

*1910-1920*                              *£250 — £350*

365 A carved oval mahogany mirror frame with bevelled-edge mirror. The scrolled carving is slightly coarse and the shape a little too elongated for elegance. It is a Victorian or Edwardian oval, not an 18th century one.

*c.1910*                              *£150 — £220*

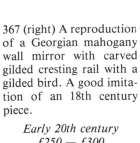

367 (right) A reproduction of a Georgian mahogany wall mirror with carved gilded cresting rail with a gilded bird. A good imitation of an 18th century piece.

*Early 20th century*
*£250 — £300*

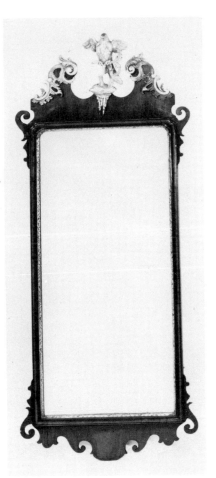

366 A straightforward 'picture frame' mirror in which a mirror has been fitted into a moulded gesso picture frame with a gilded finish. It is now very popular to fit mirrors into pine frames, obtained by stripping the gesso off frames such as this.

*1900-modern day*                    *£180 — £250*
                                     *Pine £40 — £80*

368 Walnut wall mirrors, of early 18th century design, from a manufacturer's catalogue of the 1920s. They have bevelled plate mirrors but not the gilded inner moulding to the frame which is an adjunct to value.

*1910-1930      £150 — £250*

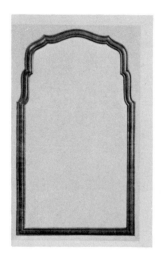
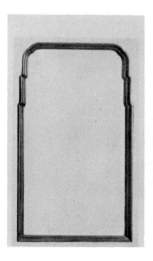

369 Reproductions of early 18th and late 17th century wall mirrors. The left-hand two mirrors are walnut-framed versions of simple Queen Anne styles, whilst the two on the right, with their deep 'cushion' moulded surfaces around the mirror and shaped cresting boards, are more sophisticated reproductions of walnut-veneered and moulded 'cushion' mirrors of the 1680-1720 period.

*Early 20th century*                     *Two on the left £70 — £100*
                                          *Two on right £150 — £250*

## MIRRORS — cheval

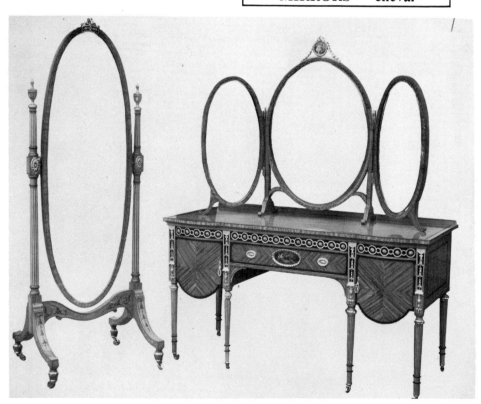

370 A satinwood cheval glass in the highest 'Edwardian Sheraton' manner, with its accompanying dressing table and (separate) dressing mirrors. The decoration is painted and gilded with classical motifs in the French Empire manner, and the whole effect is one of great elegance.

*1900-1920*                                      *£300 — £450*

371 A walnut 'cheval' mirror in the 'Queen Anne' style. Actually cheval mirrors date back to the start of the 18th century, but to find an original one like this would be a very rare event. Mirrors of this type can be safely recognised as reproductions.

*1910-1930*        *£100 — £200*

372 (left) A circular dressing mirror on a segmented pumpkin-style base. Similar designs occur in Smee's catalogue of 1850 and as far back as King's of 1830.

*1840-1865*              *£100 — £200*

373 (right) A typical mahogany dressing mirror of a design made from 1845 until the 1880s. The scrolled supports and rather heavy flat base with semi-circular plinths at each end are characteristic.

*1850-1890*              *£30 — £50*

374 Three typical early 19th century designs of dressing mirrors made in the early 20th century. The central mirror is a shield-shaped 'Hepplewhite' design which has been much reproduced; it has three small drawers in the serpentine-fronted base.

*1910-1930*
*Central mirror £80 — £140*
*Others £30 — £60*

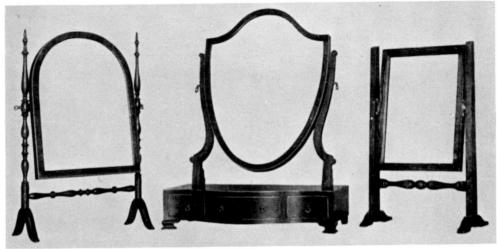

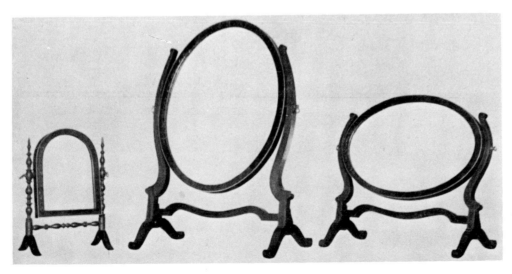

375 Three more reproduction mirrors, copying early 19th century designs, of a very popular type.

*1910-1930*              *£30 — £60*

# PINE FURNITURE

Pine was used for all kinds of furniture, so that in some ways it should be shown in most sections of this book. However, it has become customary for pine furniture to be a separate part of the antique trade, with specialist shops catering for this very popular furniture, which has been available at very economic prices for the bargain hunter. Better quality pine furniture is now quite expensive, however, fetching prices equivalent to some mahogany pieces. On the whole the most prevalent pine furniture to be found in shops is carcase furniture — chests, desks, cupboards and so on — and tables and dressers for the kitchens which it so cheerfully furnishes. This section reflects this trend.

376 (right) A pine cupboard which could be used as a dresser or bookcase, with diagonal planking to the lower doors as approved by Talbert, Eastlake and other Gothic reformers. The two drawers below the glazed upper doors lead one to believe that the piece was equally at home in the kitchen as in the library.

*c.1880*                                         *£350 — £450*

377 (left) A 'Lancashire' pine dresser base with panelled door and three drawers below the top, with its shaped back and shelf. 18th century style brass handles with back plates have been substituted for the original knobs.

*1840-1880*                                       *£140 — £180*

378 A pine bureau of a type originating early in the 19th century and remaining on manufacturers' catalogues almost to the end of it. Very often originally sold in stained or painted finish; now inevitably stripped and waxed.

*1820-1885*
*£180 — £250*

379 A heavy side or dressing table in pine with turned finials below the top corners and thick turned end supports. A design which was used for many years.

*1840-1880*                                       *£80 — £120*

380 (above) Straightforward pine chests of drawers of a type made in huge numbers, particularly in the 1870s and 1880s. That on the right has its original white china knobs, whereas the left-hand example has been prettified with modern reproduction brass plates of 18th century design.

*1860-1900*                                      *£80 — £120*

381 (right) A Wellington chest and a rather tall chest with sunken 'military' handles. The Wellington chest is not made of pine but of satin walnut, which has been stripped, bleached and waxed to a pale yellow colour. The other chest on the right is pine and has the unusual feature of a single handle for the top drawer, whereas all the rest have the normal two.

*1840-1880*           *Wellington chest £150 — £200*
                              *Other chest £90 — £140*

382 (left) Two pine dressing chests of a type very popular around the turn of the century. Many have had the mirrors removed to leave useful low chests but there seems to be a recognition lately that the mirrors really are quite useful. Also shown under Dressing Chests as 293.

*1890-1920*                                      *£80 — £130*

383 (right) A reproduction pine refectory table on four solid turned legs with heavy connecting stretchers. The top is made of three heavy thick planks and has a 'bread board' end locking the planks together.

*20th century*        *£400 — £650*

384 (above) Pine kitchen tables of late 19th/early 20th century manufacture. That on the left is of Pembroke type with flaps supported by 'butterfly' gates underneath. The table on the right is more solid and of more traditional kitchen design. Both have a drawer in the end for cutlery.

*1890-1910*                    *£50 — £90*

385 (right) A dining table from Percy Wells c.1920, intended for small houses. The top of the table was intended to be large — five or six feet long — made of deal and with square or tapered legs with chamfered edges. The tenon joints were pinned through the leg to add to strength. The ends of the top were rounded and the top was not 'thicknessed up', i.e. made to look thicker by the addition of a frieze, but left as shown. This is a happy design, robust, well-proportioned and very functional.

*c.1920*                    *£50 — £90*

386 A kitchen table and two chairs designed by Percy Wells c.1920. The table is made of deal and has square tapering legs, since 'turned legs increase the work of dusting' and cost more than a plain taper. Wells believed that this plain but pleasant table, with its drawer for cutlery in the end, was well-proportioned enough for dining as well as kitchen use.

*c.1920*         *£30 — £50*

387 A pine kneehole desk on turned feet. The centre door has an arched panel and there is a useful complement of drawers.

*1840-1870*         *£280 — £340*

388 (above) A large dresser with diagonal planking to the doors in the lower half as approved by Talbert, Eastlake, etc. The bevelling and square joints of the shelves and centre upright in the top half also reveal Reformed Gothic influence.

*1870-1890*         *£550 — £700*

389 (left) A large pine dresser-cum-display cabinet with pillared supports to the top half, which is much more imposing than the very mundane bottom half. Would the man who turned out such an elegant double-pillared top with break-front and deep cornice really have put it on so ordinary a base with such lamely-framed doors? And no bottom moulding or plinth to balance the top? Surely not.

*1890, perhaps*         *£700 — £850*

# POT CUPBOARDS

390 (left and right) Two pot cupboards of a design to be found in Smee's catalogue of 1850 and still, again, in Shoolbred's of 1876. Suitable for conversion to all kinds of uses.

*1850-1880*  *Square £40 — £70*
*Round £70 — £120*

391 (right) A typical bedside cabinet design current from 1850 to 1880. This version is in walnut.

*1850-1880*  *£30 — £55*

392 (above) Walnut bedside table-cum-pot holder with a marble top. Cleverly scalloped design on octagonal base.

*c.1870*  *£65 — £100*

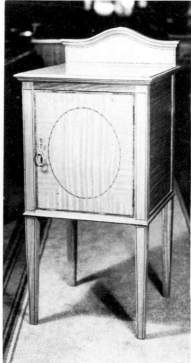

393 (left) Two satinwood bedside cabinets/pot holders of Edwardian taste stimulated by 'Sheraton' trends of the time.

*c.1900*  *£40 — £80*

# SETTEES, CHAISES-LONGUES AND SOFAS

A bit too comfortable for the likes of architect-designers, the settee and sofa attracted less design attention of the 'progressive' sort between rococo and art nouveau. The general commercial manufacturer was left to provide comfortable seating of this sort and did so, often of a buttoned and overstuffed nature. Settles (q.v.) were another matter and the production of some settle-like, art nouveau settees was a feature of the turn of the century.

The value of old settees of the completely upholstered sort is nowadays dependent, obviously, on condition and upholstery as much as style. Chesterfields tend to be sought after as a perennially popular form and have been produced and reproduced in large numbers from their inception to the present day.

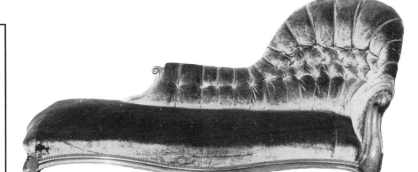

394 (above) A Victorian rococo single-ended settee or chaise-longue in the style so popular in the 1850s and made on to the 1880s. The buttoned upholstery gives it a luxurious appearance and the walnut cabriole legs are suitably over-scrolled to impress.

*1850-1880*        *£450 — £750*

395 (left) A more developed settee, again in walnut, with buttoned back upholstery and rococo curves which are so exuberant as almost to parody themselves. The legs and arm supports are carved with doubly-accentuated scrolls and with leaves. Like much Victorian rococo furniture, it is designed more for effect than for heavy wear, but one cannot help admiring the sheer confidence of the maker.

*1850-1880*        *£700 — £1,000*

396 Typical chaise-longue, with matching chairs, of a type made from the 1880s onwards, with turned legs, solid construction and turned-spindle gallery along the back. Covered in an imitation leather.

*1880-1910*        *Chaise-longue £150 — £180*
*Suite of chaise-longue, two easy and six single chairs £600 — £700*

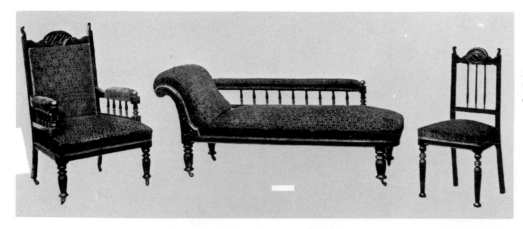

397 A slightly later suite with spindled galleries to chaise-longue and armchair.

*1890-1910*
*Chaise-longue only*
*£150 — £200*
*Suite of nine pieces*
*£600 — £800*

398 A chaise-longue, tub easy chair and single chair of a type made from c.1890 onwards. The curvy legs are a forerunner of the 'Louis' style popular in the early 1900s.

*1890-1910*
*Chaise-longue only*
*£180 — £250*
*Suite of nine pieces*
*£700 — £900*

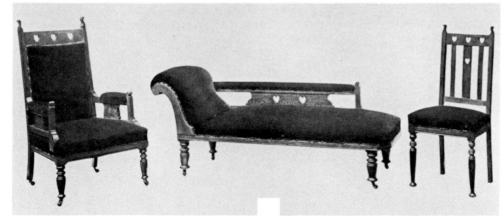

399 A commercial 'art nouveau' chaise-longue and easy chair, with single chair of a suite. The 'art nouveau' bit is from the cut-through heart shapes but, since the legs remain rotundly turned throughout (and not square section as normally done with art nouveau), it is a commercial gesture rather than a genuine design.

*1890-1910*
*Chaise-longue only*
*£150 — £250*
*Suite of nine pieces*
*£600 — £800*

400 A fully upholstered chaise-longue and easy chair with attendant 'arty' chair. The upholstery is of c.1910 velvet in a contemporary design.

*1900-1910*
*Chaise-longue only*
*£180 — £300*

401 (above and above right) Fully upholstered settees appear prominently in manufacturers' catalogues of the 1850s onwards. The chesterfield sofa is one of the enduring types but possibly appeared later. By the 1870s fully buttoned chesterfields are visible in the catalogues of Shoolbred and others. The examples shown here are from later catalogues, but that on the right is a typical example of the breed.

*£350 — £700*

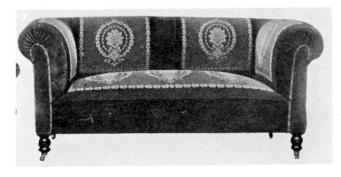

402 A selection of six chesterfields from 1900 to 1930 showing variations in coverings over the period.

*1900-1930*                    *£350 — £700*

403 An 'art nouveau' settee-settle inlaid with stylised flowers. The bowed sides are slatted above the upholstered arms and the square feet have castors inset.

*c.1900*                                    *£1,000 — £1,500*

404 A mahogany corner settee with an arm rest with turned column supports at one end. An odd 'art nouveau' piece designed for some special corner.

*c.1900*                                    *£250 — £350*

## SETTEES — drop arm

405 The drop-arm settee appears to have lost favour recently. There was a time when the pull of a lever could transform a settee into a piece of reclining furniture. Three versions are shown here, two of chesterfield type and one shaped one on square tapering legs.

*1900-1920*                                    *£300 — £550*

# SETTEES — 'reproduction' styles, 1890-1930

406 (left) A rather splendidly-covered 'French' style settee with gilded frame with gesso decoration.

*1860-1890*          *£600 — £900*

407 (below) An ebonised sofa with an inlaid panel in the back. The piece is made in a style derivative of French and dimmer traditions, with a hint of the Prince of Wales' feathers thrown in this part of the suite of drawing room furniture. The overall effect is rather flimsy.

*c.1890*          *£250 — £400*

408 (above) A 19th century English reproduction of a French sofa, made with considerable skill and expertise. One of the great difficulties with the classic French designs from Louis XIV to Louis XVI is the fact that they have been so much reproduced and so accurately. Even now, Italian and Spanish workshops, as well as the French, are turning out Louis XV chairs on a grand production scale.

*c.1890*          *£700 — £1,100*

409 (right) An 'Edwardian Sheraton' settee with a buttoned back and turned front legs. There is a characteristic inlay in boxwood and ivory in the centre of the top back seat rail, and inlaid boxwood stringing lines in the mahogany frame.

*1890-1900*          *£200 — £350*

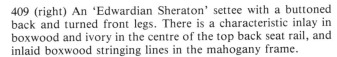

410 A settee and a day bed in walnut with much twist turning to meet the demand for 'medieval' furniture. The styles are, in fact, more attuned to Restoration furniture than the 'Elizabethan' taste they were intended to satisfy.

*1900-1920*  *settee £150 — £200*
*day bed £100 — £150*

411 A walnut two-back settee and easy chair with curving moulded cross-stretchers connecting the legs, which end in scrolled, folded feet. The legs are a fair emulation of William-and-Mary styles and the silk tapestry upholstery was a quite expensive fabric.

*1910-1920*  *settee £120 — £200*

412 A three-back settee with carved English walnut under-frame in the style of 1670 Restoration furniture, covered in silk tapestry.

*1900-1920*            *£250 — £400*

413 (above) A three-back carved walnut settee with caned panels in the backs and a caned seat. A fairly accurate copy of a type of 1670-1680 with bold turning in double bulbs to the front stretchers; scrolled, folded feet; well-swept arms ending in scrolls and elaborately-carved top rails. A good quality piece but more decorative than utilitarian, so not very expensive.

*1900-1920*            *£300 — £450*

414 (left) A mahogany settee with a caned seat and caned oval back panel with a painted crest. It is carved with 18th century motifs in the Adam-Sheraton manner and is on square tapering legs with block feet.

*1910-1920*            *£250 — £400*

415 (below) A bergère settee and armchair in a style of French Hepplewhite derivation with painted decoration and an oval central painted panel to the settee, depicting a recumbent scantily-clad lady attended by cherubs on what looks like a sea shore. The contemporary fabric on the upholstery is somewhat fussy for the classical design and decoration of the structure.

*1910-1930*            *settee £200 — £350*

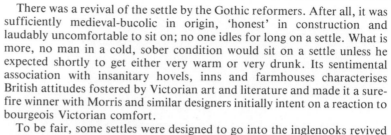

There was a revival of the settle by the Gothic reformers. After all, it was sufficiently medieval-bucolic in origin, 'honest' in construction and laudably uncomfortable to sit on; no one idles for long on a settle. What is more, no man in a cold, sober condition would sit on a settle unless he expected shortly to get either very warm or very drunk. Its sentimental association with insanitary hovels, inns and farmhouses characterises British attitudes fostered by Victorian art and literature and made it a sure-fire winner with Morris and similar designers initially intent on a reaction to bourgeois Victorian comfort.

To be fair, some settles were designed to go into the inglenooks revived by Norman Shaw and other domestic architects but by the 1920s the settle seems to have become a piece of hall furniture with a seat that lifted as a lid to give access to a coffer-like compartment under it — to house boots? slippers? bottles? — and no one was expected to sit waiting in the hall for long.

416 The full treatment — a William Morris settle with profuse painted decoration. Note the detail of the coved top shown below.

*1885-1895*        *£4,000 — £8,000*

417 An oak and beaten copper settle in the 'art nouveau manner, using the copper plaques with tulip forms associated with Arts and Crafts furniture of what is now thought of as English art nouveau. The hinged seat lifts to give access to the coffer-like interior.

*1900-1910*        *£250 — £300*

418 (right) The classic reproducer's version of the oak settle, not very much removed from the original 17th century piece except that the panelling is symmetrical, modern in construction and rather austere. The seat lid lifts up to give access to the storage space in the lower half. The price is affected by the now very high price of the original period version.

*1900-1915*                                    *£150 — £250*

419 An oak settle or 'monk's bench' which is, in fact a chair-table, since the back of the seat tilts over to form a table top at an inconvenient height. There is a hinged lid in the seat, giving access to the storage space. The front is panelled with a shaped apron. Not now very desirable — the storage space was intended for rugs, presumably used when travelling.

*1900-1915*                                    *£40 — £60*

420 An oak seat or settle from Percy Wells, 1920. An object which seems to have taken a long time dying and which was used as a 'hall seat', although Wells claimed it could be used just as well in a living room, with the addition of cushions to make it comfortable. Not a cheap piece and an interesting example of the survival of older forms of furniture, modified slightly in design, well into the 20th century. Wells pointed out the lack of 'meretricious ornament' which dignified the piece and the simple strap carving.

*1920*                                          *£135 — £200*

# SIDEBOARDS

By 1860 the sideboard had followed the evolution of styles in much the same way as other Victorian furniture, with a few slight differences. From its original, Adam form, it became a heavier, end-pedimented piece made in sub-classical, usually Grecian, style with a heavy, drawered top connecting the two end pediments. Sometimes there was a gap between the two pediments, under the top like a large 'kneehole', sometimes this area was cupboarded in. The latter type, with cupboards, has been much preferred by the antique trade and is more expensive. Rococo forms of sideboard exist, but rococo seems to have been more used for the chiffonier or side cabinet intended for the drawing room. The dining room furniture was far more serious, heavier stuff, more suited to the grave atmosphere to be associated with eating. Chairs followed a similar pattern.

Commercial production continued to supply these heavy dining room sideboards and even carved oak versions in emulation of the famous 'Chevy Chase' piece, smothered with carved fauna and comestible fruit and vegetables, until the end of the century. In the 1870s the return to 18th century reproductions saw the re-introduction of the Adam form and the 'Sheraton' or late 18th/early 19th century versions of it. In Edwardian times some satinwood reproductions were made — even the William Morris Company produced them — which were quite good versions of the originals, with the possible exception that inlaid or painted decoration in the Adam style tended to be overdone. These pieces are elegant, however, and are now quite highly priced.

The Gothic reformers, the 'art furniture' boys, Godwin, the Arts and Crafts Movement, the Cotswold crafties and the 'garden city socialists' in their various turns, despised 'commercial' sideboards almost more than any other form of furniture. To them the Victorian sideboard epitomised the vulgarity, the parvenu tastelessness, the crass greed and the ostentation of the rising middle class Philistine. They reacted to it in their various ways and the commercial manufacturers copied them all. Talbert produced his 'Pet' sideboard in Reformed Gothic. Godwin, with William Watt, produced his celebrated Anglo-Japanese versions, one of which is in the Victoria and Albert Museum. The art furniture boys laid the ebonising on thick, spindled the galleries, coved the tops and painted some of the panels in startling colours which contrasted with the ebonising. The Arts and Crafts Movement went in for plain oak surfaces, flat-capped tapering columns, art nouveau beaten copper hinges with heart shapes and fretted holes in weepy shapes. The Cotswold crafties and the garden city socialists really didn't like to get involved with sideboards at all. They preferred dressers, since dressers are more in the medieval tradition, more 'country' than the wealthily-inspired sideboard. The sideboards they produced are often really a form of dresser base or an adaptation of a simple dresser form or, in the case of Gordon Russell, a universal pedestal desk/dressing table principle used for sideboards.

By the 1900s the medieval oak taste had set in with a vengeance as well as the desire for 18th century reproduction. From about 1900 onwards the sideboard became subject to an extremely varied number of styles, some of them employed all on one piece. But the 'Jacobethan' mass production of post-1918 was probably the major feature and sideboards were produced to go with the bulbous-legged 'refectory' or draw-tables of cheap stained oak. The other rival would be a walnut 'Queen Anne' style which was probably slightly more expensive. Gradually overtaking them came a style now referred to loosely as 'art deco'; modernistic, round-edged and 'streamlined' with a few carved motifs stuck on.

## SIDEBOARDS — 1860-1900

This section shows the contrast in styles to be found in English furniture over what was a very short period of forty years. From straightforward 'Victorian' mahogany, through Reformed Gothic, Aesthetic, and Anglo-Japanese is a very drastic transition of styles, but that is what was made, at least by those in the 'forefront of taste'.

421 A sideboard in mahogany with the low-arched panels which came into fashion in the 1840s and which continued to be made until the 1880s. This is a very simple version with serpentine shaping to the drawer fronts.

*1840-1880*                    *£150 — £250*

422 Another mahogany sideboard with classical pillars and cheap leaf-and-scroll carving around the mirror back. It is a type which, with dismemberment and reassembly, can be turned into a 'Regency' chiffonier by the adept converter.

*1840-1860*                                    *£150 — £250*

423 The characteristic early Victorian chiffonier-sideboard made from the 1840s onwards. Panelled doors with the flattened arch and 'feather' mahogany figures; ogee moulded drawer fronts; acanthus leaf carving; solid plinth and carved curvy back. Cheaply made and mass produced; hated by all 'progressive' designers.

*1840-1880*                                    *£150 — £250*

424 A walnut sideboard in the severer lines of the 1860s with a galleried top incorporating turned spindles and finials. The inconsistent use of oval mirrors in conjunction with rectangular ones is disconcerting. The burr walnut veneer is inlaid with boxwood and ivory stringing lines and formalised marquetry and there is a white marble top.

*1860-1880*                                    *£300 — £500*

425 A carved oak sideboard of a design inspired by the 'Chevy Chase' type exhibited prominently in the mid-Victorian period. Carved oak (or mahogany) sideboards with large quantities of unfortunate fauna and flora suitable for gastronomy carved upon them became quite popular, even if expensive. It was a taste that continued despite the disapproving scowls of the Gothic reformers and subsequent progressives.

*1850-1880*                                    *£800 — £1,600*

426 A Bruce Talbert 'Pet' sideboard made by Gillows in oak with characteristic carving of foliage, use of spindles in galleries and a quotation above.

*c.1873* £1,500 — £2,200

427 An oak sideboard designed by Charles Eastlake (see *Hints on Household Taste*, Plate XI) showing the restrained version of Reformed Gothic with angled planking and incised mouldings so characteristic of the type. There is a carved quotation in Latin across the top.

*1870-1880* £1,400 — £1,800
*Photo: Courtesy Jeremy Cooper*

429 (right) A simpler Reformed Gothic sideboard with tongued-and-grooved planking but with a pierced gallery above with four carved seated lions.

*c.1880*
£400 — £700

428 Another oak sideboard showing a wealth of angled tongued-and-grooved planking and a carved panel of birds as well as painted panels in the Aesthetic Movement manner.

*1870-1880* £600 — £900

430 An ebonised Anglo-Japanese sideboard designed by E.W. Godwin (q.v.) of a type now exhibited in the Victoria and Albert Museum. Godwin's use of Japanese design is discussed elsewhere on pages 27 and 28. What is important from a value point of view is that the piece exhibits a design trend towards the Modern Movement in its vertical and horizontal lines. It is thus, as a milestone in furniture history, that its value to suitable museums is extremely high.

*c.1877*                    *£20,000+*

431 Another ebonised Anglo-Japanese sideboard by E.W. Godwin. A buyer paid nearly £7,000 for this piece at Sotheby's Belgravia in 1978. Why so much less than the previous example? A telling point this — because it does not so clearly exhibit the horizontal and vertical lines which point the way to the designs of the Modern Movement. It is thus of less interest to museums as a furniture history milestone, even though it has great value as a piece by Godwin.

*c.1877*                    *Value: see above*

432 A characteristic Aesthetic Movement sideboard of ebonised and mahogany construction with a coved top with spindled gallery. The bevelled-edged mirrors, panelled construction and turning are all typical.

*c.1880*                    *£500 — £750*

433 (right) A rosewood inlaid sideboard which shows how, at the end of the century, the return to 18th century styles had affected commercial production. Indeed, this piece shows traces of the 'Victorian Queen Anne' style or 'bracket-and-overmantel' style in the broken pediment and design of the upper half, yet it still has traces of a spindle-turned gallery and 'pot board' bottom shelf of the Aesthetic Movement. Yet the inlaid decoration is 'Adam' or 'Sheraton' and the piece would now be sold as 'Edwardian Sheraton'. It is not quite as late as the Edwardian styles shown in later pages of sideboards, as the reader may note, however.

*1890-1900*                              *£450 — £500*

434 An odd oak sideboard of slightly progressive-cum-quaint associations in design. (The wavy-line pierced gallery is the 'quaint' part.) The photograph gives it a slightly asymmetric look, which is misleading. Probably by Liberty's.

*1890-1900*                              *£450 — £600*

## SIDEBOARDS — 1900-1920

435 Six typical late Victorian/Edwardian sideboards of a type made in oak or walnut of the straight-grained American type. Mostly identified as to period by the bas-relief carving in panels or on pediments, and the use of a modified classical pediment so dear to the Edwardian heart. The common features to all are the large back mirrors with columns either side, drawers with cupboards under in the lower half and panelling to the cupboard doors, achieved by either fielding or mouldings.

*1900-1914*                                                    *£250 — £400*

# SIDEBOARDS — art nouveau and progressive, 1890-1915

436 (right) A sideboard-cum-side cabinet of interesting art nouveau decoration on serpentine bracket feet. Included here because surely the lower half, with its three central drawers and flanking cupboards, dictates that it was intended as a sideboard. The piece has rather astonishing inlaid 'tulip' decoration with whip-lash curves, and the two high side cabinets on the top half flank a much more conventional glazed cabinet of shorter dimensions. The glazing bars have an additional curved bar each side of the central panel, as though the designer was tired of the verticality of the construction and wanted to relate something to the sinuous inlays. Note the interesting use of diagonally-chequered stringing lines which give an Arts and Crafts touch.

*1890-1900*                      *£900 — £1,600*

437 A mahogany sideboard of interesting design which combines a traditional English form with the use of inlays of 'whip-lash' art nouveau floral decoration. The canted glazed side-cupboards are a design associated with Liberty's, who espoused art nouveau and 'quaint' furniture enthusiastically.

*c.1900*                      *£300 — £450*

438 An almost aggressively art nouveau oak sideboard, more on the Continental lines of the style than the British. The sides of the lower half, with their protruding tapering stiles in the 'Eastlake' manner, are broken by the sinuous curves of carved floral decoration. The bronze hinges, handles and applied tulips are over-decorative and there is a good deal of ostentation about the amount of carving used all over. Notice the flat capped finials along the top — a feature used by Voysey but emulated in a way he disliked intensely.

*1900-1910*                      *£500 — £800*

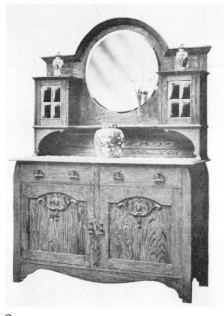

a

b

c

d

e

439 Commercial adaptations of the 'art nouveau' style in sideboards, from the use of leaded-light cupboards (an English favourite, this) to the simple, rather bankrupt embellishment of heart-shaped frets and added fretted curves on (e). Notice the tapering upward columns on the sides of the top of (b), ending in flat caps — a feature of Voysey's designs for several pieces of furniture.

*1890-1914*          *(a), (b), (c), (d) £200 — £450*
                              *(e) £150 — £250*

440 (right) A nice small oak sideboard which shows how the principles of the Arts and Crafts movement could be applied to a piece with restraint. The bronze panel let in to the back with its typical spade shapes and the carved 'trees' in the door panels relieve the almost altar-like severity of the pointed uprights.

*1900-1914*          *£120 — £200*

## SIDEBOARDS — reproduction, 1880-1930:
## 18th century and early 19th century mahogany

The revival of 18th century designs in the 1880s saw the return of the traditional 'Georgian' mahogany sideboard which has persisted as a favourite ever since. Conceived by the Adam brothers around 1760 as a rather extended range of table and pedestals, the form has been modified until very suitable for most dining rooms. The traditional pillared dining table, mahogany chairs and sideboard are such a deeply-ingrained English form that even now the industry producing modern reproductions must account for a large proportion of all dining furniture sold in the British Isles.

441 The sideboard almost as Adam originally saw it in 1760. Two pedestals flanking a table with a wine cooler under it. The pedestals have urn-shaped vases lined to take iced water for drinking and hot water for washing silver. The pedestals could be used as plate warmers and wine storage (cellaret) if required. The central table has a high brass rail behind it. This is a faithful Edwardian reproduction — they were good at making these. The pedestals and urns are now the most valuable part for their decorative qualities.

*1900-1920*                    *without cellaret £1,400 — £2,500*

442 The next stage on from the Adam design. The end pedestals have been integrated with the table. The urn-shaped vases (or is it vase-shaped urns?) remain. The brass gallery is more decorative. A reproduction of a 1780-1800 design.

*1900-1910*                    *£1,000 — £1,500*

443 Now comes a third stage. The pedestals have been attenuated into two cupboards on square tapering legs and the central table has a deep drawer. The vase-shaped urns have gone. Almost the accepted form of Georgian sideboard so beloved of the reproducer.

*1900-1910*                    *£600 — £1,000*

444 (right) An integrated half-circular version where the deep cupboards either side and the central section are now the same depth. To fill in the space, the central section has a drawer and a large space below it. A high quality version would have a tambour shutter to draw across this space.

*1900-1920*                    *£400 — £800*

445 (left) A mahogany sideboard of shallower proportions without the shelf under the central section. A very faithful copy of a style popular around 1790-1820 but made a hundred years or more later. The bow front contains a central drawer and kneehole flanked by two deep cupboards. The boxwood stringing lines provide an elegant and restrained decoration appropriate to the spirit of a simple George III piece.

*1900-1930*                    *£250 — £400*

446 (right) A mahogany bow-fronted sideboard now much shallower with little difference in depth between central drawer and cupboards. In this case the decoration is a little more elaborate than that of 445, but the proportion is clumsier, partly due to the thick legs and partly to the over emphasis on the thickness of the top.

*1900-1930*                    *£200 — £350*

# SIDEBOARDS — reproduction, 1890-1930:
## 'Queen Anne' styles leading to 'burr walnut bedappled'

It is not quite clear when the return to 18th century designs led to a thirst for 'Queen Anne'. Certainly the cabriole leg was used on dining chairs before the end of the century. This feature, on sideboards, seems to have been a bit later — say in the 1890s — but the design seems to have gathered popularity until its heyday in the 1930s. (See also 'burr walnut bedappled' in Design Data Sheets, page 37.)

The 'Queen Anne' style, exemplified by the use of the cabriole leg, should not be confused with 'Victorian Queen Anne' which was a more Palladian, William Kent-ish architectural style with triangular or broken pediments popular around the 1870s and 1880s for cabinets. The Queen Anne of Edwardian times is nearer the real thing, using cabriole legs and fiddle-shaped splats for chairs. It is not a pure style, however, and is distinct from exact reproductions of Queen Anne pieces.

447 (left) An oak sideboard (also made available in mahogany at the time) whose only real claim to Queen Anne pretensions lies in its thin, weakly-designed cabriole legs. There is the high back of Victorian taste and the large central mirror. The open central section was rather hopefully called a cellaret by the makers but the bowl placed within it in the photograph has unfortunate connotations of night-time use.

*1900-1910        £100 — £140*

448 (right) A second variety of oak sideboard where, again, the only claim to Queen Anne styling is in the weak front cabriole legs.

*1900-1910        £100 — £140*

449 The back is lower and squarer and someone has had the idea of attaching a carved embellishment to each door. Otherwise only cabriole legs give it the Queen Anne name, but at least they are on the back as well as the front.

*1900-1915                    £100 — £140*

450 Still coming down, the back is lower and the flat-capped uprights of art nouveau contrast somewhat with the Queen Anne cabrioles. Made in mahogany; not a Queen Anne wood. The popular Edwardian semi-circular central arch has had a Queen Anne carved 'shell' put in it — very appropriate.

*1900-1915                    £80 — £120*

451 A burr walnut sideboard, this time with a short modern back and on paw-footed cabriole legs with rather bulbous toes and shell-carved knees. The carving on the door mouldings and the top edge has a rather machine-reproduced look about it.

*1920-1940*　　　　　　　　*£120 — £200*

452 (above and right) The back has gone entirely and the form is distinctly modern reproduction. Two variants on the figured walnut Queen Anne style sideboard showing a return to the 'dressing table' shape.

*1920-1940*　　　　　　　　*£100 — £200*

453 A rather fancy sideboard of a type associated with the Bath Cabinet Makers in the 1920s and 1930s. It is 'Queen Anne' with 'William and Mary' overtones and even William Kent type chamfered fluted edges. So here we go:

— The legs are cabrioles with shell carving and scroll feet introduced c.1720.
— The stretchers connecting the legs and the scrolled carved cresting rails between them are associated with the period 1680-1700.
— The oyster veneers and inlaid boxwood are c.1680-1700 but the 'feather' or 'herring-bone' banding belongs to 1700-1720.
— The canted corners with fluting are an architectural motif associated with William Kent c.1720-1730.

Oh well, why not?

*1920-1930*　　　　　　　　*£300 — £450*

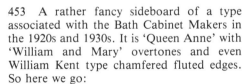

# SIDEBOARDS — reproduction, 1890-1930: 'Jacobean' oak varieties

The 'Jacobean' style was popular well before the onset of the standard 'Tudor' dining room of the 1920s and 1930s. By the 1890s the popularity of medievalism had brought out a surge of 'old oak' manufacture. Commercially produced sideboards of the period simply reflect the desire to satisfy this trend.

454 (right) An oak sideboard of almost standard top design, except that the prevailing columns on either side of the mirror are twist turned. The drawer fronts are moulded and the door panels are fielded. The piece has a pot-board stretcher beneath and bulbous turned front legs in imitation of Elizabethan types.

*1900-1910*                              *£300 — £450*

455 (below right) Again a variation of standard design at the top but this time the cupboard doors are on either side of three central drawers and have geometric mouldings on them. Twist-turned legs, with square section stretchers, end in bun feet.

*1900-1910*                              *£200 — £300*

456 (above) A lower back without mirror — the start of the move towards lighter furniture for lower ceilings, perhaps. Actually a piece designed in emulation of a court cupboard, with a dominating, over-hanging top moulding with big, turned finial suspended under each end. Doors and panels are geometrically moulded and, in the cases of the two end doors, fielded as well.

*1900-1915*                              *£300 — £400*

172

457 A very interesting oak sideboard in an amalgam of 'Olde English' styles with inlays in boxwood (or holly) and a darker wood, perhaps ebony. The geometrically moulded drawer fronts and back panels are 'Jacobean' in design, emulating oak chests of the 1670-1690 period and the bobbin-turned double-column front legs and stretchers are taken from lighter furniture of the 1680-1700 period, such as gatelegs and side tables. The inlays, with the Prince of Wales' feathers motifs, are quite 19th century in inspiration and the checked boxwood-and-ebony stringing lines are of the type favoured by designers of the 1890s to 1920s, such as Waals and the Barnsleys, although such lines were used in the 18th century also. The occasional square sections in the bobbin turning of the stretchers are an erroneous diversion, since such square sections, in the original period, were only used at the joints, not left stranded in mid-section such as these. The thumb-nail moulding round the serving top and its lower moulding outlines are quite authentic to the 17th century but the top to the back incorporates a dentillated moulding which is mid-18th century in design. It is not clear whether the piece is meant to be stained in any way when finished, but the implication is not, since it was the fashion, 1880-1910, for such 'back-to-Elizabeth I' designers to leave the natural wood unstained and simply to wax polish it.

*1900-1910*                    *£400 — £800*

458 (left) The 'lower' move continued. This time the back has been cut down to a simple one with the central arch characteristic of Edwardian furniture. Geometric mouldings and applied split balusters decorate the surfaces. Large turned bulbous feet/legs in Elizabethan style.

*1900-1915*                    *£180 — £250*

459 (below left) An oak sideboard in the 'Jacobean' manner, incorporating moulded drawer fronts, twist-turned legs and stretchers, scrolled pierced carving in Restoration style and a low arched back as favoured by Edwardian fashion, but getting ever lower.

*1900-1920*                    *£120 — £200*

460 (above) The back has almost gone, preparing the way for the simple Jacobean styles of the late 1920s and 1930s. Otherwise similar decoration to previous examples.

*1900-1925*                    *£80 — £160*

# SIDEBOARDS — chiffoniers

461 The 'vulgar' chiffonier, much hated by 'progressive' designers did not really change very much over a period of fifty years as these three examples from a 1910 catalogue show. Add a bit of spindled gallery; the occasional broken pediment or turned pillar; a bit of machined carving in bas-relief but leave the basic format the same, seems to have been the rule of thumb. Some versions — the better ones — are in solid mahogany; some — the nastier ones — are cheap thin veneer on a cheap deal frame, or even stained deal.

*1910*                                        *£65 — £130*

# SIDEBOARDS — hybrid, 1900-1930

From 1900 to 1930 the sideboard was also subject to a mixture of styles being applied to one piece. A small selection of such hybrids is shown here to illustrate how there are quite a large number of pieces which defy classification into an accepted stylistic nomenclature.

462 (right) A veneered walnut sideboard incorporating panels of burr veneer and herringbone inlaid lines with crossbanding around them. The piece is a mixture of William and Mary walnut styles — in the turned and octagonal faceted legs and in the cross-stretchers — and a curious sort of Edwardian Sheraton in the bowed central front drawers with satinwood technique in the laying of veneers. The back, with its central arch, is pure Edwardian design but the scrolled carving stuck — no, applied — under the cabinet section is late 17th-century-inspired. One has a strange sensation, looking from the top gradually downwards, of rushing back in great jerks through 130 years of styles, starting at 1910.

*1910-1920*                    *£100 — £300*

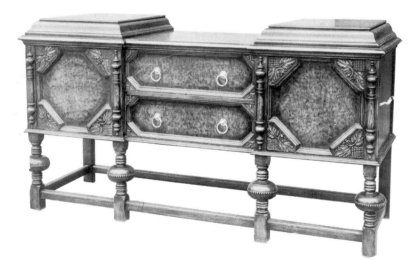

463 An oak sideboard in the 'Tudor' or 'Jacobean' manner, exhibiting late 17th century decorative characteristics but early 20th century in both design and execution. The 17th century decorative features are the applied split balusters on the vertical frame, the 'bun' turnings, the stretchers, and the geometrically moulded door and drawer panels. The carving is modern, the 'gramophone cabinet' pedestal top is out of period, and the proportion quite distinct.

*1910-1930*                    *£150 — £250*

464 A mahogany sideboard, heavily carved with acanthus leaf, floral and fruity decoration, standing on cabriole legs with ball-and-claw feet. The back incorporates a broken pediment, also with carved similar decoration. The uncarved panelled surfaces are quarter veneered symmetrically and the doors are either curved or serpentine in shape. The piece represents quite an accomplishment of the cabinet-maker's art and draws upon mid-18th century motifs. It is, however, entirely 'improved reproduction' in form and spirit, belonging strictly to the period of its manufacture.

*1920-1940*                    *£100 — £350*

465 (right) A burr walnut sideboard on carved cabriole legs and incorporating a carved frieze below the central drawers of Restoration inspiration. The feel of the piece is intended to be 'Queen Anne' in design — i.e. with burr walnut, cabriole legs, cross-banded panels and so on, but the very low back gives it quite a modern appearance. Much reproduced.

*1920-1930*                                  *£150 — £250*

466 (below) A cabinet on cabriole-legged stand, surely intended for use as a sideboard. Why else the six square deep drawers and the central cupboard, with its scrolled apron? The figured walnut was probably used throughout the suite to which it belonged.

*1920-1935*                                  *£100 — £200*

467 (right) A side cabinet in feathered mahogany and of ogee shaping, mounted on short cab-riole legs with shell carving on the knee. Ig-noring the 'Queen Anne' legs, the piece is mid-18th century mahogany in inspiration but the band of blind fretted carving across the front has a very machine-made look about it.

*1920-1940*
*£100 — £200*

## SIDEBOARDS — 'modern', 1920-1930

In this section a number of interesting designs which are quite modern in spirit and technique are illustrated. They are mostly by 'famous' designers with perhaps the exception of Percy Wells. In due course it will be possible to produce further illustrations as more research and identification work is carried out — the real detection work is required to identify those pieces made by original designers of international stature.

468 A solid walnut sideboard by Gordon Russell with yew cross-banding, ebony stringing lines and ebony-and-yew handles. The design, with its latticed back gallery is very akin to one of Gimson's. The use of square stretchered legs on pedestal desks, dressing tables and other pieces is characteristic of Gordon Russell.

*c.1924*                                  *£350 — £550*

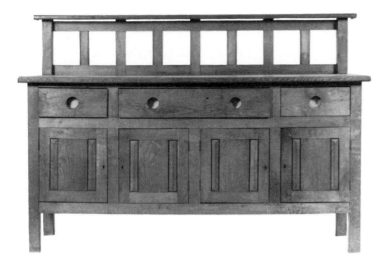

469 A dresser designed by Frank Brangwyn — yes, he did design furniture as well as paint — with a slatted back gallery and panelled doors. A nice piece, more suitable for sideboard respectability than kitchen dresserdom.

*c.1925*                                    *£300 — £500*

470 A mahogany sideboard designed by J. Henry Sellers, rather characteristic of his tendency to place a lower shelf beneath a severely linear, almost Sheraton, upper structure with drawers with black stringing lines at the edges. Designed en suite with the dining table shown as 515.

*c.1925*                    *£100 — £200*

471 (left) An oak sideboard designed by Percy Wells c.1920, of a very simple conception. Its origins can be traced to the art nouveau example, 440, and before that to washstands and similar functional pieces. No drawers were fitted, to reduce cost. The chair next to it shows art nouveau origins as well, but of the English rectilinear version, not the curvaceous Continental model. Indeed the lower half of the chair owes more to country Sheraton design than anything else.

*c.1920*                                    *£40 — £80*

472 (right) A mahogany sideboard designed by Percy Wells, c.1920, which has wandered across the line from his definition of a dresser. The central cupboard was designed to be able to take bottles (not of alcohol, surely? HP sauce, perhaps, or ketchup) and the shelves at the back for books or china. Actually, a very functional piece which fulfils Wells' desire to keep proportion small for the small rooms involved and to meet a real storage need. It is interesting that he has retained turned front legs on this piece and the original Welsh concept of the pot-board below. He has also embellished the piece with two curved arches to the top but hastens to say that "the article would be just as useful without the little ornamentation which has been introduced" and then, in the same sentence, simply gives into weakness by lamely confessing that "utility, though first, is not the only thing to consider in furnishing a home." Revisionist tendencies, Wells! To the salt mines!

*c.1920*                    *£80 — £120*

# STANDS — hall (for coats, umbrellas, etc.)

The hall stand is an interesting piece of furniture for sociological reasons as much as stylistic ones. What did the first hall stand look like? Are there 18th century hall stands? There are boot racks and planks full of pegs or nails from the 18th century but the hall stand in its form shown on these pages appears to be a 19th century development, something which grew along with the increase in halls in houses. For the 18th century cottage, there was rarely a hall. One simply fell down the front step into the living room, hitting one's head on the beams. For the wealthier gentry, external clothes and hats would be taken away by a servant. No, it must have been the same, well-worn old Rise of the Self-Sufficient Middle Class, with its entrance hall or passage, where coats, hats, boots and umbrellas were parked, which gave rise to the need for this piece of furniture. Now the hall stand is gradually dying, too wasteful of space to compete with pegs on the wall, too profligate in providing for far too many umbrellas and walking-sticks made redundant by the motor car. The hall itself is under attack, shrinking and shrinking so as to provide more space allocation to the living areas within a house.

And yet one retains an affection for the old hall stand. Its ability to tear a sleeve if passed by in a hurry; its mirror, uselessly hidden behind coats hanging upon it; its metal umbrella trays, full of cigarette ash; its cunningly-designed centre of gravity, so sure to allow it, when the last heavy coat was hung upon it, to tip forward and crush one beneath it; these are the things that one misses. And the sheer exposure of leaving a good coat or umbrella open to view on the hall stand of a populous family house; the certainty that it or they would be missing when needed.

What really makes the hall stand a thing of the past is the modern desire for neatness and order. A hall stand covered in coats, mackintoshes, umbrellas and galoshes or wellies is a muddlesome, unlovely sight. The clothes closet, with its hangers and the vacuum cleaner, has supplanted it. There has been a recent vogue in America to use wardrobes (q.v.) in place of a stand, thus hiding the offensive paraphernalia away and causing yet another container shipping boom, this time from the old wardrobe market. The Habitat brigade have gone in for bright red bentwood stands (q.v.). The hall stand of seventy years ago is having a job to avoid the hatchet; mark this progression of them before they disappear, leaving only the odd survivor in the museums.

473 A hall stand which was produced in oak or mahogany, incorporating a broken pediment, finials and two cupboards either side of the umbrella stand. More 18th century in conception but typically Edwardian in its use of the bas-relief carved panels and, indeed, in that particular form of broken pediment, which was used on so many pieces of larger furniture.

*1900-1915*                    *£80 — £100*

474 (left) A combination hall stand incorporating a broken pediment and a cupboard on bulbous carved 'Elizabethan' legs. A piece to meet the prevailing fashion for carved oak furniture, with lion masks, scrolled dolphin-like objects and acanthus leaves all proclaiming the maker's open-minded attitude to the use of motifs from widely different periods. The temptation to break this piece up for use as various bits of other pieces of furniture would be strong to the modern producer.

*1900-1915*                    *£80 — £100*

475 (right) The influence of art furniture upon hall stands. A mahogany or walnut model with a gallery of turned spindles above the mirror and a tiled panel above the glove box. Alas, however, a broken pediment surmounts the whole, reverting to a classicism Collcutt and Godwin would not have liked.

*1900-1915*                    *£40 — £60*

476 (left) A slight genuflection towards the progressive movement here. Look at the flat top with its deep-set moulding; the hooped umbrella rail; the tapering frontal leg under the brush drawer. Art nouveau has had a look in. The round bevelled mirror, though practical, is out of keeping with the shapes preferred by the art nouveau designers, however.

*1900-1915*        *£25 — £40*

477 (right) A bamboo hall stand in which the maker, confronted with a surplus of material, has joyfully cross-strutted the framing and added fanciful chinoiserie grilles around the mirror.

*1900-1915*        *£30 — £45*

479 (left) An oak hall stand with an oval mirror and a brush box, surmounted by a broken pediment on top. It is 6ft.9ins. high and the top pegs ensure that only the master of the house or a particularly lanky offspring can reach the hats parked up there. A wise precaution: many a Homburg has been smashed due to juvenile collisions with the hall stand.

*1900-1915*        *£20 — £30*

478 (below) A hall stand, available in oak, mahogany or American walnut, of slightly more developed form. The bevelled mirror has beaten metal panels over and above it and the front legs are turned.

*1900-1915*    *£25 — £35*

480 (right) A simple hall stand with a narrow mirror, a glove box and two umbrella holders, with metal trays. The fretted corner brackets are decorative, an attempt to disguise its appearance as a guillotine frame.

*1900-1915*        *£15*
*(No, not a penny more)*

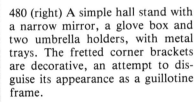

481 (left) An oak hall stand for umbrellas, with a glove box or drawer. The carving is typical of late 19th/early 20th century 'oakiness' with a lion mask and scroll-and-leaf forms. Now something of an anachronism and ripe for conversion into a console table of some sort.

*1900-1915*        *£45 — £75*

# STANDS — occasional

Nos. 484-491 show a selection of perennially favourite stands for plants, busts and other ornament requiring elevation, from a manufacturer's catalogue of 1900-1910.

484 (left) An oak palm stand on four long legs with shelf stretcher.

*£25 — £40*

485 (right) An inlaid oak jardinière of a type often made with decoration of hanging chains.

*£70 — £100*

482 (above) A burr walnut 'jardinière' or pot holder in the French rococo manner. With typical ormolu mounts on the 'knees' of the cabriole legs and a brass gallery rail around the top.

*1860-1880      £150 — £250*

483 (right) An Edwardian 'art nouveau' pot stand in oak, flimsily made but with typically-shaped gallery or railing in the lower half. Ideal for Art pottery display.

*1900-1915      £30 — £50*

486 (left) An ebonised turned pedestal suitable for a bust of Mr. Gladstone.

*£100 — £180*

487 (right) A mahogany palm stand on a tripod base in mid-18th century style.

*£120 — £180*

488 (left) Ebonised turned pedestal of heavy dimensions and of distinctly 19th century design.

*£100 — £180*

489 (right) A more conventional ebonised fluted pedestal of 18th century classical design.

*£150 — £220*

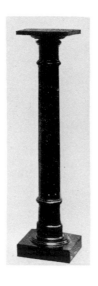

490 (left) A mahogany palm stand similar to 484 but inlaid with 'Sheraton' stringing and decoration.

*£40 — £70*

491 (right) Another palm stand based on a jardinière design.

*£60 — £90*

# STOOLS

492 (left) The universally-recognised Victorian piano stool on rococo tripod base with scrolled decoration. The seat has been re-covered and the buttoning is not as deep as the original would have been.

*1850-1875*          *£150 — £300*

493 (right) A similar but higher quality base adds value to this square stool with needlework seat.

*1850-1875*          *£200 — £300*

494 (right) A scrolled rosewood stool with a woolwork covering. The 'X' supports at each end are connected by a turned stretcher with baluster shaping.

*1850-1870*      *£120 — £220*

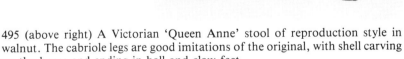

495 (above right) A Victorian 'Queen Anne' stool of reproduction style in walnut. The cabriole legs are good imitations of the original, with shell carving on the knees and ending in ball-and-claw feet.

*1890-1900*                      *£175 — £250*

496 (left) An oak reproduction 'joint' stool with a top which is hinged like a lid to allow access to a storage space under, concealed by the frieze, which is carved with an arched pattern. The column-turned legs and square stretchers are correct copies of a 17th century type. Joint stools were much reproduced from about 1900 onwards and still are. To an oak fancier they provide the only means of having a low occasional table, suitable for coffee-cum-armchair use, which is in period with oak furnishings. Due to the high price of originals, these are pretty expensive too.

*1900-present date*                      *£90 — £140*

## TABLES — centre pedestal

Not all the tables in this section started out life as dining tables by any means. Many were intended as centre tables or for occasional use, but the modern collector, with more modest space and size of household, is happy to adopt them for dining. Indeed, many of the large extending tables used in Victorian dining rooms are now more suitable for boardrooms or for those who entertain many people at a time than for modern dining purposes. These larger tables are dealt with in the section, TABLES — dining.

497 (above) A walnut centre table on four scrolled supports which are themselves on four scrolled cabriole legs. A very popular design in the 1850s. (Smee's catalogue shows an almost identical table, 1850.) Now perhaps regarded as a high-point of scrolled Victorian rococo, whose exuberance and frivolity snap their fingers at the stolid, classical dourness of the other prevailing styles. Not designed constructionally for heavy use but a splendid example of the genre.

*c.1860*                 *£700 — £900*

498 (above) An oval walnut centre table on a centre turned support and four carved scrolled supports on an X-shaped platform which is, in its turn, on four scrolled feet. This elaborate base is of a type popular in the 1850s and 1860s.

*c.1860*                 *£400 — £650*

499 (right) A circular walnut centre table on a gadrooned baluster column and three scrolled rococo legs. The top is veneered in sections of burr walnut whereas the base is solid. A design popular in the 1850s but still offered by various manufacturers in modified form to later dates.

*1860-1870*              *£500 — £700*

500 (above left) An oval walnut table on a four-column base with four scrolled feet and a finialled circular central section. The top is inlaid with box-wood stringing and stylised foliage marquetry. Stylistically derived from the 1850s and 1860s but more likely to have been made twenty years later when this four-column version of the base was very prevalent in commercial catalogues such as C. & R. Light.

*1865-1885*                                    *£350 — £500*

501 (above right) A walnut oval breakfast table inlaid with stringing lines and a centre marquetry panel. The designer has adopted a belt-and-braces approach in using both a centre column and four smaller supporting columns rising from the curved legs. Similar designs occur in catalogues of the 1860s to the 1880s.

*1860-1885*                                    *£175 — £300*

502 (above) A circular rosewood table in the George III manner, with a broad satinwood banding to the top and satin-wood panels in the curving legs support-ing the turned centre column. The top is veneered in two matched halves of figured rosewood and the quality of execution is very high.

*1910-1930*            *£600 — £900*

503 (right) A mahogany two-pedestal rectangular dining table of Georgian design. The column-turned supports end in four curved reeded legs with brass paw castors and the table is a straight-forward reproduction of one of the most popular forms of English dining table.

*1920 to present day*       *£300 — £500*

> The centre pedestal table was quite a favourite of the Reformed Gothic designers who adapted Pugin's models to their own ideas. The use of structural timbers of more architectural configuration was a hallmark of the type and some of the really high-quality, roof-beamed versions in oak with inlaid tops are now very expensive collectors' pieces.

504 (right) An oak centre pedestal table with a tip-up top which is of Puginesque design, although probably not by him. The use of the grotesque carved animals' heads and the heavily-pillared centre column, more like stonework than wood, is typical of the use of Gothic design. Note the carved edge of the table top, with its Gothic-Islamic motif. Possibly intended as a library table and of the mid-Victorian Gothic style transitional between fanciful Regency 'Gothick' and the severer Reformed Gothic of the 1860s.

c.1850                                    £500 — £700

505 A typical Reformed Gothic octagonal centre table using 'revealed' construction and an architectural structure to the base, following Pugin's example. The top is inlaid and the joints are pegged, with ebony 'dowels' to mark them, reiterated in the decoration of the frieze. Note also the carefully-designed handles.

c.1865                                    £700 — £900

506 Another, very popular, design of octagonal table in which the Reformed Gothic style is marked by the heavy crossed stretchers on the base on which the four turned column supports stand. These crossed stretchers curve downwards to form feet and, in this case, have a further stretcher between them at the base of each column.

c.1865                                    £500 — £750

507 An octagonal walnut centre table on four column supports and a structural stretchered base ending in shaped feet. The piece has all the hallmarks of Reformed Gothic design: turned collars on the columns, ebonised for emphasis; moulded stretchers connecting the heavy central crossed base with its chamfered edges; incised Gothic trefoil motifs.

1865-1870                                 £450 — £650

508 Put here for contrast and instruction, this octagonal pitch-pine table is still 'Gothic' in style but is probably ecclesiastical in origin and taken from a chapel or a church. The base looks a little out of proportion with the top.

1870-1880                                 £150 — £200

509 A mahogany expanding dining table of a type often thought of as mid- or even late-Victorian but whose legs belie the later dates. Although the constructional form was used later, it originated in the 1830s and 1840s. These legs are of a bulbous-and-baluster turning with collars, more popular initially in the 1840s than in the 1880s and later, where one might be tempted to place this piece. The examples of 1880-1910 incorporate the top bulb but the lower turning is straighter or tapering, less of baluster form. The piece does highlight the difficulty of dating Victorian furniture, however, since the use of this form of baluster at a later date is always possible.

*1840-1890*                    *£200 — £400*

510 Another large expanding Victorian mahogany dining table, this time with semi-circular ends which can open to receive up to four flaps. The tapering reeded legs are of a design popular in the 1830s, featured by Smee in 1850 and still used in variant form in the 1880s.

*1835-1885*          *£600 — £900*

511 An example of the previous type of table, adapted in style to be more 'Sheraton' in appearance, with square tapering legs and inlaid stringing lines. Available originally in a size 7ft. long by 4ft. wide.

*1890-1915*                    *£200 — £350*

185

512 Four examples of the leg styles available in the late Victorian and Edwardian era. From almost-art-nouveau through 'oak' to 'Queen Anne'.

*1890-1915*                                                                 *£25 — £45*

513 A mahogany extending dining table which, with its three leaves inserted is 2ft. 6ins. wide by 10ft. long. The top, shown here without leaves is slightly serpentine in shape and has an edge decorated with a blind fret. The tapering rectangular legs have patera at the top and carved husk decoration. An example of 18th century Georgian designs used on a modern table.

*1900-1925*
*£500 — £750*

514 A cabriole leg dining table which can be extended on the 'draw table' principle (i.e. by extra leaves under the top), thus combining stylistically 'Queen Anne' shaping with a 16th century construction. From Maurice Adams.

*c.1926*                    *£120 — £200*

515 A mahogany dining table designed by J. Henry Sellers (1861-1954), an Arts and Crafts Society architect-designer who tended to produce expensive furniture with Edgar Wood. The top is banded with ebony and, clearly, the ends are detachable in the manner of the 18th century 'D' end dining table. Designed en suite with the sideboard shown as 470.

*c.1925*                    *£250 — £350*

# THE DRAW-EXTENSION TABLE
## FOUR ALTERNATIVE DESIGNS—JACOBEAN, QUEEN ANNE, ADAM, AND MODERN WITH SQUARE BALUSTER LEGS

516 Illustrations from *The Woodworker* magazine of 1928 showing four versions of the popular small draw-extension table used in small houses, with subsequent directions for the do-it-yourself enthusiast on how to construct the piece. Interesting that the lower left version was entitled 'modern' in design at that date, even though its square baluster legs and cross stretchers are derived from traditional tables.

*1920-1940*          *£20 — £40*

FIG. 1.—JACOBEAN DRAW-EXTENSION TABLE.
SIZE, CLOSED, 4 FEET BY 3 FT. 6 INS. SIZE EXTENDED, 7 FEET BY 3 FT. 6 INS.

FIG. 2.—QUEEN ANNE EXTENSION TABLE IN WALNUT.

FIG. 3.—OAK EXTENSION TABLE WITH SQUARE BALUSTER LEGS.
NOTE.—THE SIZES OF ALL FOUR TABLES ARE AS IN ELEVATIONS, FIGS. 5a AND 5b.

FIG. 4.—ADAM TABLE IN MAHOGANY.

The vogue for the medieval led to a tremendous rise in demand for oak furniture of suitably aged appearance from the 1880s onwards. 'Old oak' refectory and dining tables might be made up from old pieces (just as 'coffers' might be made from three-panel carved bed-heads) or simply reproduced new and 'aged' by various processes. It was not always the intention to deceive, nor is it so now.

We show a small selection here to show how close some versions came to the original and to advise the reader to be warned; old reproductions of good quality are worth about half the value of the originals.

517 (above) A really heavy oak reproduction refectory table with primitive lion-mask carving, on six enormous carved bulbous legs. The sheer quantity of oak involved would make such a table enormously expensive to produce today, let alone the question of the carved decoration.

*1890-1920*                    *£2,000 — £2,500*

518 (left) A simpler oak 'draw-leaf' table on four bulbous carved legs. The stretchers have been jacked up off the ground by the addition of four square 'feet' at a later stage. The top has been panelled across the length which is considered a less attractive proposition by the trade.

*c.1900*                    *£900 — £1,300*

519 A rather unattractive oak 'refectory' table which looks as though it has been 'made-up' from old pieces but the legs have turning which is plain and rather modern. No attempt has been made to 'age' the stretchers by wearing down the edges.

*c.1920*          *£400 — £650*

520 (left and below) Two oak draw tables from Maurice Adams, 1926. Straightforward, quite well-designed reproductions made to satisfy a contemporary taste for 'Jacobethan' dining rooms. Of quite high quality construction.

*1926*                                                    *£100 — £250*

521 A cheap oak dining table, of the 'draw' type, on a two-pillar base derived from 'Jacobethan' but carefully 'modernised' to provide those streamlined, curved surfaces beloved in the late 1920s and 1930s. Note how the traditional turned 'bulb' on the supports have been modified into ribbed shapes of no particular beauty. The surface was originally dark-varnished with a sticky cheap 'French polish' which has become badly scratched.

*c.1930*                                                    *£15 — £25*

The most successful form of dressing table seems to have been one with drawers in pedestals on either side. Indeed, the walnut reproduction desk shown in the Desk Section (No. 326) is, in fact, a copy of a kneehole dressing table of c.1700 (but see the *Price Guide to Antique Furniture* for all about that). The simpler the design, very often, the more successful it was. Apart from the pedestal type — which has been much converted into desks — the 'lowboy', with its two deep drawers and one central shallow one, on cabriole legs, is the very other popular form.

The advent of built-in bedroom units has meant the demise of many large pedestal dressing tables but the smaller, prettier ones have survived as whimsical occasional tables, even in the bedroom. These smaller tables tend to be the more highly valued.

522 (right) A dressing table of a type made by Holland & Co. in satin ash with ebony stringing lines and brass gallery rails above the upper drawers. Perhaps made en suite with the 'Wellington' chest 303. A high-quality piece of furniture in a simple pleasing style.

*1850-1880*                    *£300 — £450*

523 (below) A dressing table designed by Owen Jones for Eynsham Hall, Oxon, in 1873. In fact, Shoolbred's catalogue of 1876 shows examples very similar in design. This piece is in a pleasant, light wood and the stringing lines and neat black knobs contribute to an easy formality of design which is wholly missing from much furniture of the period. Unfortunately many dressing tables of this sort have had the top section removed to cater for the enormous trade in pedestal desks.

*1870-1880 (for unattributable piece)*        *£300 — £400*

524 (below right) A rather more 'Victorian' mahogany version of the preceding examples, with scrolled carved supports to the shaped mirror. The pedestals are bow-fronted and the descent from simple clean lines to something less tasteful is clearly illustrated.

*1850-1880*                    *£180 — £300*

525 Down further we go, into semi-rococo ugliness. The oval mirror is all right but the rest is fairly unpleasant and extremely wasteful of space. Apart from the central drawer the frieze is totally unused and probably 'false' while as for the legs and bottom shelf . . .!

*1850-1880*            *£80 — £120*

526 An oak dressing table and mirror to match with revealed construction in the manner approved by the Gothic reformers. The arcaded painted decoration is in keeping.

*c.1870*         *for table and mirror £300 — £400*

527 (left) A painted dressing table which has borrowed something from the art furniture brigade in its design and perhaps something from Regency 'bamboo'.

*1890-1900*
*£90 — £120*

528 An inlaid mahogany dressing table in the Sheraton manner, owing something to the Carlton House writing table in the curving design of the centre section which leads, in the upper storey, to two drawers. The inlays incorporate shell and swag motifs.

*1900-1910*           *£200 — £300*

529 An inlaid mahogany kidney-shaped dressing table in the 'Sheraton' manner, depending on a late 18th or early 19th century original design but somewhat over-decorated by the Edwardians.

*c.1900*                                              *£1,000 — £1,500*

530 A Liberty's dressing table in the 'art nouveau' style in its more straight-line English variety. Usually made en suite with an accompanying washstand (see 608).

*c.1900*                                              *£200 — £300*

531 (right) A mahogany dressing table of 'art nouveau' design with inlaid decoration and square tapering legs ending in round feet.

*c.1900*
*£120 — £180*

532 A walnut 'Queen Anne' dressing table of a type known as a lowboy. One of the most popular and pretty pieces from the walnut period of 1710-1730 and much reproduced. See the *Price Guide to Antique Furniture* for several original examples.

*c.1925*                    *without mirror £180 — £300*

533 (left) Another walnut dressing table of 'Queen Anne' style but which is immediately apparent as a reproduction version, not true to original proportions, from the long cabriole legs. The previous example is much more true to the original.

*c.1925*
*without mirror*
*£80 — £120*

534 A 'William and Mary' style dressing table, so termed because of the inverted-cup turning, bun feet and shaped stretcher of the base. Not the correct proportions for a period piece.

*c.1925*                    *£80 — £140*

535 One of Maurice Adams 'original' designs, successful commercially in the 1920s and 1930s, based on 'Queen Anne' styles. This example is in figured walnut but mahogany versions were also available. An entirely post-1920 interpretation of Queen Anne and quite identifiably 20th century.

*c.1925*                    *£70 — £120*

536 A veneered walnut dressing table, with wardrobe-chest to match, on cabriole legs with shell carving to the knees. Anyone seeking to comprehend why 20th century burr walnut furniture is so far in appearance from the early 18th century pieces it vaguely emulates should look at the sheer fussiness of the figure in these veneers and the confusion it generates even when laid in matched symmetrical sheets.

*1920-1940*          *table only £100 — £140*

537 Lacquered versions of 'Queen Anne' (right) and 'William and Mary' (left) dressing tables. There was a revival in lacquer furniture (often on a blue ground, but also red and black) in the 1920s which now has a market in the interior decoration business.

*c.1920*                                                                                   *either version £100 — £160*

538 A walnut veneered dressing table and wardrobe with drawer above. Very much post-1918 in design, with solid pedestal bases emphasised by dark applied mouldings, no separate feet, square unembellished edges and solid square ebonised wooden handles. The central drawer of the dressing table has been replaced by a glass shelf. Quite what the drawer above the wardrobe was used for is not certain — Something the Children Must Not Find, perhaps?

*1920-1940*                                                                                   *table only £100 — £150*

## TABLES — gateleg

The gateleg table was a great favourite of the 17th and 18th centuries. It did not die out in the 19th century but continued in other forms, like the Sutherland (q.v.) table.

During the last quarter of the 19th century, however, it was back to the Good Old Days for gatelegs, as with so many other forms of furniture. The oak gateleg was back in its late 17th century form, to meet the prevailing demand aroused by the medieval and 'Olde Englishe' taste.

539 (left and below left) Two oak gateleg dining tables of good reproduction of styles of 1670-1720. The top example has the column turned legs — here slightly balustered — which were put on many conventional tables of this sort at the end of the 18th century. The lower table features spiral or twist turning to the legs (but not the stretchers, which are left square) which met 'Elizabethan' taste, but which in fact dates back to 1670-1690. Both tables have a give-away feature for those anxious to identify period. Both have a deep 'thumb-nail' or ovolo moulding around the top. This is not a feature generally to be seen on period tables and was much used by reproducers from 1900 onwards.

*1900-1920*

*top £120 — £180*
*bottom £150 — £200*

540 (right and above right) Two occasional gateleg tables of small size from Maurice Adams. The top one, with a robust end 'gunbarrel' column, emulates an early small gateleg of the 1670s. The lower example is more conventional with column turning and square stretchers. Both have a 'thumb-nail' top edge moulding. They are intended for lounge or drawing room use, not for dining.

*c.1925*

*top £30 — £45*
*bottom £45 — £75*

541 A white deal gateleg table of the old type of construction shown by Percy Wells c.1920. Wells liked the enduring virtues of the gateleg — the design variations to top and leg, the convenience of storage, and use at half or full dimension. Unlike the Pembroke, it is hard to top over because of the leg support, but this very virtue is a drawback since the legs get in the way of the sitter. Wells proposed to overcome the objection of the low foot rails by setting them back from the legs and projecting the top further over. He also proposed a change to the gate system to avoid halving the leg or the long rail. He shows drawings of the new system but not a photograph. The table shown above is 5ft. long by 2ft.10ins. and, as Wells points out, is much more costly to construct than a plain kitchen table of the same size on four legs.

*c.1920*                                            *£50 — £75*

542 (above) Two small lacquered gateleg tables for occasional use, in the chinoiserie style much revived in the 1920s. The legs are extremely slender and the tables are clearly not designed for much other than ornamental purposes.

*1920-1930*                                         *£50 — £90*

543 (right) A reproduction oak gateleg table with twist-turned legs. Note the flat stretchers without any form of incised moulding and the heavy 'thumb-nail' or ovolo moulding around the top. Both features are strong indications of a reproduction as against a 17th century original. Made in a fairly cheap oak and stained or semi-French polished to give a darkened aged appearance, but this finish is apt to scratch or chip off. This type of table was made in enormous quantities. There are container loads of them available from trade shippers specialising in this kind of furniture but recent activity has increased the price, which in 1979 was a standard £38 or so.

*1920-1930*                                         *£60 — £90*

196

544 A walnut centre table inlaid with a marquetry panel and with ormolu mounts. Very similar to the writing table 582 and, again, made in a French Louis XVth style of perennial popularity. Not as high quality as 582 but nevertheless still a well-made and very decorative piece.

*1860-1890*                                                    *£800 — £1,400*

545 A centre table of Reformed Gothic character from Blackmoor House, c.1872 (see *British Furniture, 1880-1915* by Pauline Agius, pl. 74). Possibly designed by the Manchester architect, Alfred Waterhouse, a friend of Norman Shaw. Waterhouse designed for Blackmoor, starting in 1869 and imitated Shaw's 'Old English' style as used at Leyswood, which still had Gothic features such as the gate tower. The table is interesting in its construction of Reformed Gothic style and structure but incorporating half-and full suns of Japanese character and the spindled gallery. The move from Gothic to Anglo-Japanese can be perceived.

*c.1870*                              *£500 — £750*

546 An interesting ebonised centre table with a turned spindled gallery connecting the end supports which are pierced and carved with stylised flowers and leaves. Of Reformed Gothic character but with later developments in the carving.

*1880-1890*                 *£500 — £700*

197

547 A mahogany centre table of rather Continental design on spun brass cup feet of a type associated with W.A.S. Benson, a designer for Morris & Co. who specialised in metalwork. The same feet are used on furniture attributed to the firm of J.S. Henry (see *British Furniture, 1880-1915,* by Pauline Agius, p.94, pl.112).

*c.1900*                                                          *£190 — £240*

548 An occasional centre table of octagonal shape, in rosewood, with eight turned legs and a centre column joined by stretchers radiating from the centre. An arcaded apron also joins the legs. Possibly by Collinson & Lock.

*c.1880*                                                          *£250 — £350*

549 Another spider-like centre table with a moulded top edge, by Morris & Co. Made in mahogany. The firm produced several similar designs, available in mahogany or fumed oak.

*c.1900*                                                          *£200 — £300*

550 A six-legged mahogany centre table by a commercial firm of general furnishers. Clearly the type was popular up to 1914. Also available with only four legs.

*c.1910*                                                          *£120 — £180*

551 (right) A 'Chippendale' version of the octagonal mahogany centre table on eight legs. This time the radiating stretchers are pierced and fretted with scrolled work. The top edge is gadrooned.

*1910-1920*                    *£180 — £240*

552 (below) An oval 'Sheraton' style centre table on four tapering square section legs ending in castors and connected by curved stretchers emanating from a central finial. The top is inlaid and crossbanded; there is satinwood banding and boxwood stringing around all the normally approved edges.

*1890-1900*                    *£550 — £750*

553 (below) Two small occasional tables of the type ideal for coffee or tea drinking in the sitting room. On the left, a scalloped top with dished edge and chinoiserie decoration, mounted on carved cabriole legs ending in hoof feet. On the right, a segmented feather-veneered mahogany top with crossbanding, mounted on cabriole legs ending in hoof feet, with a lion mask carved at the top and a frieze also carved in basrelief with scrolls and shells. Nothing, of course, like these two tables was made in the periods from whose styles they have borrowed. The 20th century had advanced both comfort and practicality in arriving at the dimensions, then it has imposed the most marketable styles associated with high quality on to the design.

*1920-1940*                    *£90 — £180*

199

The tripod table is an 18th century invention, probably developed from candle stands. It is still one of the most popular occasional tables and has been much reproduced.

554 A Victorian version of the tripod table, in walnut, with a scalloped edge in emulation of the 18th century 'pie crust' edge. The shaping of the column is unmistakably mid-19th century and the use of the finial below the column is also characteristic of mid- to late Victorian furniture. The shaping of the legs is also not that associated with Georgian tripods.

*c.1870*                                    *£50 — £75*

555 A mahogany tripod table with a brass gallery rail around the circular top and decorative scrolled supports in addition to the centre column.

*1900-1920*                              *£120 — £200*

556 Mahogany tripod tables with moulded rims, fluted columns, reeded vases — spiral to the left, straight to the right — and elegant legs carved with acanthus leaf decoration. Essentially straight reproductions of 18th century tripod tables but looking shorter in proportion and the tops of a greater diameter than the period originals would probably have had. Good quality pieces, though.

*1900-1920*                              *£90 — £160*

# TABLES — side and card

557 An ebonised card table decorated with inlaid boxwood stringing and marquetry. The canted edges of the folding top are banded with burr walnut. The four-pillar support and curved feet with arched cross-stretchered design topped by a vase-shaped finial is typical of mid-Victorian popular designs dating from 1860 onwards to the 1880s. C. & R. Light (1881) and Wyman (1877) show similar tables. The stylistic origins are French-classical and had a considerable vogue but ebonised furniture is not now a widespread taste. The inside top surface is baize lined.

*1860-1880*                                    *£175 — £250*

558 An octagonal walnut card table with folding top, of similar date to 557. This time the base has more scroll decoration, leaning towards rococo stylistic ornament. Again a popular mid-Victorian style but more acceptable to modern taste due to the presence of walnut rather than ebonising, so a higher price to be expected.

*1860-1880*                                    *£250 — £400*

559 A burr walnut card table with a rectangular top inlaid with ebony stringing lines and boxwood marquetry. This table has again got four turned columns supporting it but the base has been designed in end-standard or trestle fashion instead of a central platform. There is, again, the popular mid-Victorian turned finial, echoed in reverse below, between the end columns and the base is quite crisply carved with classical elaboration.

*1860-1880*                                    *£350 — £550*

560 A figured walnut card table in a 'semi-Gothic' style, in which the maker has used the same principle as the previous example for construction — i.e. a double-pillar-and-stretcher base — but adapted cleverly to Gothic reformed styling in treatment with addition of some ideas of his own in the carving. A quite high quality piece probably made by a 'commercial' firm.

*1860s*                                    *£300 — £450*

561 An inlaid marquetry card table in the French 18th century manner with metal mounts. As we have shown in the Bureaux — bonheurs-du-jour section there was a considerable vogue for these high quality French pieces in the 1860-1880 period and considerable skills were involved in their production.

*1860-1885* £500 — £800

562 A mahogany side table in the Adam manner, with serpentine top veneered in segments and fluted frieze and legs. There is a central drawer in the frieze with a panel carved with a vase motif. Another example of the return to Adam classical designs which occurred in the 1880s. A rather difficult piece to place for the average collector and more likely to find an interior decorator's approval.

*1880-1900* £250 — £400

563 A satinwood table with folding top incorporating a shell inlay in the Sheraton manner. Useful as an occasional or games table with tray below and a superior example of a whole range of occasional tables with stretchers, trays or ledges below, made very popular in the Edwardian period.

*1900-1910* £200 — £300

564 A satinwood and marquetry card table in the 'High Sheraton' or Adam manner, inlaid with ribbon-tied swags of flowers on the top and frieze. The square tapering legs, ending in block feet, are also inlaid. It is a classic example of the return, in Edwardian times, to late 18th century inlaid furniture and is a high quality reproduction, only erring in its probable tendency to over-elaboration. The Edwardians often felt that they could out-perform the original inlayers and this results in an over-profuse marquetry that betrays the reproduction from the original.

*1900-1910* £500 — £700

565 A mahogany card table of half-round type ('*demi-lune*'), opening to a circular top, in the 'Sheraton' manner. The top and frieze are inlaid with marquetry showing swags of husks. The square tapering legs end in castors. Again a good example of the return to late 18th century Sheraton taste of classical type in the Edwardian period with a fairly faithful reproduction of the original 18th century type.

*1900-1910*        *£400 — £600*

566 A reproduction 'Chippendale' folding card table in mahogany, on square legs with gadrooned edges. The serpentine shaping of the top is authentic but the carving on the frieze would give rise to a query from someone seeking the 18th century original. The ribbon and carving around the top edges is also perhaps a little too bold for the original article. A high quality piece nevertheless.

*1900-1910*        *£300 — £450*

567 The oak craze personified — an oak chair-table in imitation of a 17th century piece, in which the top tilts to act as the back of the chair when it is not used as a table. The rosettes carved into the top, which appear to adorn both sides so as to be constantly visible, are not particularly in period spirit. The straight column turning of the legs and arm supports is, however, bold and laudable. A piece of convertible furniture which has always been a bit too clever by half — one can neither sit at it to eat, nor eat off it when sitting.

*1900-1915*        *£70 — £100*

568 A mahogany side table with 18th century square tapering legs, connected at back and side by an unnecessary stretcher. There is a back piece with a broken pediment. Intended as a hall table, but bordering on a washstand.

*1900-1915*        *£45 — £75*

569 (left) A mahogany reproduction 'Chippendale' card table in the 18th century rococo manner, on cabriole legs ending in ball-and-claw feet. The scrolled carving on the knees of the legs is crisply executed and so are the carved edges to the top. Just a little weakness at the ankles to identify the reproduction from the original, although colour and patina would be important indications.

*1910-1920* £400 — £700

570 (below) A large mahogany version of a side or console table with carved central lion mask and profuse carving of acanthus leaf, fruit and floral forms. The cabriole legs end in hairy paw feet. An imitation of mid-18th century console tables in the grand manner, but rather high, large and clumsy for any use other than a hotel sideboard in Eastbourne or Gleneagles.

*c.1910* £500 — £750

571 (below) A floral marquetry reproduction side table with the very difficult form of 'open-twist' turned walnut legs ending in bun feet and with a veneered cross-stretcher. The spirit of the c.1680 date it is emulating has been very carefully kept even though it is obviously brand new — look at those crisp sharp edges on the square section joints above the bun feet, and the cross-stretcher is a bit too square in section. (It should have been wider and shallower.) There is also something a bit unfinished about the rail below the drawer. The marquetry is fine quality even if a bit too bold and big in individual flower for 17th century work. Admirable, nevertheless.

*1910-1930* £700 — £1,000

572 (right) A 'William and Mary' walnut side table with turned legs incorporating inverted cup (or 'bell') forms and bun feet, connected by an 'X' stretcher. A reproduction which is identifiably modern yet reasonably close to the original in spirit.

*c.1925* £50 — £85

573 A walnut drop-leaf gateleg table of a type known in the trade as a Sutherland table (for some obscure reason). Made in mahogany or walnut (i.e. veneered in figured or burr walnut), these tables can be supported on a single turned column at each end, as shown above, or on a double column with spiral or other turning. There is an extra, thin, turned leg on a gate at each side which swings out to support the flap when open. They can be seen clearly above. The Victorians do not seem to have minded this rather unhappy lack of cohesion in leg design; the gatelegs often look like a pair of poles or walking sticks that someone has leant in random fashion against the frame under the flaps. The merit of the design is, of course, that the table, when folded, is very slim in end elevation and the whole is mounted on castors so that it can be tucked away neatly. The spiral grooving turned into the legs of the above example is often found on these tables.

*1860-1890*                                    *£140 — £190*

574 A similar design of Sutherland table in mahogany, with the same form of end columns and mounted on white castors.

*1860-1890*                                    *£100 — £150*

575 An ebonised Sutherland table which shows very clearly how undesirable ebonised furniture looks when dusty and in poor condition.

*c.1890*                                    *£30 — £60*

576 A rectangular Sutherland table with spirally-turned double end supports on a simple arched foot design. The thumb-nail top edge moulding appears on almost all the tables at the time.

*1870-1890*                                    *£80 — £120*

# TABLES — work and games

578 (right) A walnut combined work and writing table on turned end-column supports with scrolled feet connected by a turned stretcher. Under the hinged top there is an adjustable reading and writing flat covered with tooled leather, and stationery compartments on each side of this flap. The drawer pulls out to provide a fitted interior and the wooden work bag below can also be pulled out for access. The figured walnut top surface, drawer and bag are inlaid with stringing lines and marquetry. The whole piece is very similar to one illustrated in the design book of C. & R. Light in 1881 but such pieces were popular throughout the mid-Victorian period.

*1860-1885*          *£400 — £550*

577 (above) A papier mâché work table inlaid with ivory and mother of pearl in floral patterns and scrolls. The design is not unlike those of the 1830-1840 period with a baluster central column and a flat base with four scrolled feet.

*c.1860*          *£450 — £650*

579 (right) A walnut work and games table with inlaid chequerboard and backgammon board, on a twin-column end support stand with connecting turned stretcher. A type illustrated in manufacturers' catalogues up to 1885.

*1860-1885*          *£400 — £650*

580 (left) A walnut work table of a type which was introduced in the late 1850s as an urn shape, but which had settled to this funnel or trumpet variety by the 1870s. This example is inlaid with floral marquetry and stands on rather cocked-knee cabrioles with scrolled feet. The top has been inset with leather: this almost certainly means that the original marquetry top has been damaged and, to save expense, a new leather top has been fitted. Damage to the top surfaces is frequent with these tables; the veneer was very thin and was easily lifted by heat or spillage of liquids.

*1860-1880*

*marquetry £200 — £350*
*walnut £140 — £200*
*mahogany £100 — £160*

# TABLES — writing

The borderline between a writing table and a desk or bureau is sometimes hard to define. On the whole a writing table remains a table, on four legs with some drawers in the frieze, but the Carlton House version is almost a desk or bureau due to the upper structure. Here, we have followed accepted practice and, after the Carlton House version, show the simpler pieces of furniture.

581 A satinwood 'Carlton House' writing table with oval panels in the upper doors. The type appears in Gillow's cost books for 1796 and is also illustrated in the 'Cabinet Maker's Book of Prices' of 1788. Carlton House was the residence of the Prince Regent. Gillows simply describe the piece as 'A Ladies' Drawing and Writing Table'. We tend to associate square tapering legs with Sheraton, but this type of table had a considerable revival in about 1890 and is still being made to the present day. (Harrods usually stock one or two.) Readers of the *Price Guide to Antique Furniture* will know from page 258, items 942-945 that there are marquetry ones, satinwood ones, plain mahogany ones and there are even painted ones. Variations in the design are very frequent in lesser Edwardian pieces.

*1890-present day*   *marquetry/satinwood £3,500 — £5,000*
*satinwood as above £2,000 — £3,500*
*painted/inlaid mahogany £2,500 — £3,500*
*mahogany, little decoration £750 — £1,250*
*satinwood, little decoration £1,000 — £2,000*

582 An inlaid satinwood writing table in the French Louis XVth style on cabriole legs with ormolu mounts. The top surface has an inset leather area, crossbanded around it with additional inlay. The top edge has an ormolu moulding surround.

*1860-1880*                                    *£1,200 — £1,800*

583 Three writing tables in 18th century styles, using square tapering or turned legs, brass ring handles with circular pressed plates and with drawers in the frieze. The central example has small upper drawers as well. All have an inset leather top.

*1890-1920*                                    *£150 — £250*

584 Three writing tables of rather less quality. The central one is kidney-shaped and the other two are oak examples with square section legs.

*1890-1920*                                                                    *£40 — £85*

585 An inlaid mahogany writing table in the 'Sheraton' style which also incorporates an oval mirror with flanking small drawers.

*1890-1910*                              *£200 — £300*

586 An oak writing table in 'William and Mary' style, evidenced by the turned legs with inverted cups or 'bells' and the bun feet. The front stretcher has been thoughtfully omitted so as to allow the writer to get his or her feet under the table without hindrance.

*1900-1920*                              *£100 — £150*

# WARDROBES

There was a time, until recently, when all wardrobes seemed to be destined for the breakers. Built-in cupboards were replacing them everywhere. Then there was a revival in the Georgian clothes press; now wardrobes seem to be perking up, led by the export trade. It is all very baffling and involves Fashion. Wardrobes were made in all the styles of the period. Many have been broken up or exported at very low prices. Higher quality ones with veneers and inlays now seem to find a ready market, so scorn them not.

587 (left and below left) Clothes-press wardrobes of typical Edwardian type, based on late 18th century Georgian models. In walnut and oak.

*1900-1910* *£60 — £100*

588 (below right) A comprehensive wardrobe in oak. The long shallow drawers in the lower section were for trousers and were fitted with presses, a section which could be reconstructed as a folio chest.

*1900-1910* *£50 — £90*

589 Mahogany clothes press in the 'Sheraton' style with boxwood stringing.

*1900-1910* *£90 — £120*

590 Small Edwardian wardrobe with dressing chest and washstand en suite. Typical of many such sets made in large numbers in the period.

*1900-1910* *wardrobe only £15 — £25*

591 Large oak wardrobe en suite with dressing chest and washstand. Note the deep drawers under the hanging section. The inlay is of ebony and pewter.

*1900-1910* *wardrobe only £30 — £50*

210

592 (right) A veneered satinwood wardrobe suite including a shield-back Hepplewhite-style chair (solid wood) with turned legs and a bedside cabinet veneered to match the wardrobe. Note how these turned legs are painted with black stringing lines to give the impression of reeding. The floral decoration is painted and the oval medallions depicting classical figures are also probably painted although on some furniture these scenes were put on by means of a printed transfer.

*1900-1920*                    *wardrobe only £300 — £450*

593 (below) A walnut bedroom suite with inlaid boxwood stringing lines emphasising edge bandings and with 'diamond-pane' boxwood stringing decoration. Note the symmetrical pattern produced on the wardrobe doors by the veneer sheets and the vertical-torpedo shaped legs applied externally to the carcase construction of the tables and chair.

*1920-1940*                    *wardrobe only £100 — £200*

594 A dwarf wardrobe and dressing table in rather violent lacquer decoration. The wardrobe could be used by a child or might make a good cocktail cabinet. Cabriole legs and 'Queen Anne' styling throughout.

*c.1925*
*wardrobe only £70 — £90*

595 A walnut side cabinet on cabriole legs. Its doors incorporate matched sheets of burr walnut veneers which give the impression of Rorschach's ink-blot tests or some similar method of simple symmetric reproduction run amok.

*1920-1940*                *£100 — £180*

596 Another high quality satinwood wardrobe in late 18th century 'Sheraton' style, with painted decoration.

*1900-1920*                *£350 — £500*

597 A lacquered and painted wardrobe with a scene depicting something from James Hilton's Shangri-La, perhaps.

*c.1920* £300 — £450

598 A simple, pleasing wardrobe designed by Percy Wells, using three-ply for the panels and deal for the frame construction. The design goes right back to the panelled simplicity of 17th century models, but in trying to achieve lightness the result may have been flimsy.

*c.1920* £10 — £25

599 Back to Chippendale — a mahogany wardrobe with 'feather' figuration, blind frets, pagoda-ish top and serpentine bracket feet. Ignore the chair.

*c.1920* £350 — £450

600 The veneer figurations on this bedroom ensemble defy description.

*c.1925* *wardrobe only £200 — £300*

601 'Burr walnut bedappled' at its height — not to be viewed with an early morning hangover.

*c.1925*                    *wardrobe only £200 — £300*

602 Maurice Adams version of 'burr walnut bedappled' — on his splayed 'Quannepplewhite' feet and with panels of matched, quartered veneers on serpentine front and side panels. Wow!

*c.1925*                    *£200 — £300*

603 A wardrobe suite including bedside table, dressing stool and chair. The base of each piece is emphasised by a band of darker veneer which, on the wardrobe and bedside table, is repeated above the doors. The central door of the wardrobe is decorated by using a development of veneer 'quartering' of symmetrical sheets but incorporating geometric diamond shapes and vertical and horizontal lines. The overall effect of the very clean lines is extremely modern.

*1920-1940*
*wardrobe only £50 — £85*

# WASHSTANDS

604 This mahogany washstand from the *Price Guide to Antique Furniture* showed how the Georgian mahogany type came to develop into that which we associate with the Victorian era — a plain back, turned legs, wooden drawer knobs. Subsequently the Victorians improved the breed by adding marble or tiles to the surfaces liable to get wet and by omitting the sides and adding towel rails — as on the next examples.

*c.1860*                                                    *£60 — £90*

605 Mahogany washstand with marble top and back. Inlaid stringing lines in box and ebony.

*c.1900*                              *£35 — £50*

606 Slightly more 'artistic' washstand with marble top and green tiled back. Inlaid stringing lines in box and ebony. Note the towel rails.

*c.1900*                              *£40 — £60*

607 (left) Oak washstand on turned tapering legs. Green tiled back, marble top, integral wooden towel rails.

*1900-1910*                                                    *£35 — £50*

608 (below left) A Liberty's oak washstand en suite with a toilet or dressing table (530). The back is inlaid with pewter tulip heads above a canvas flap. The surface for the washbasin is of lead and there are cupboard doors below.

*c.1900*                                                      *£100 — £200*

609 (below right) A corner washstand illustrated by Percy Wells c.1920. The design is basically 18th century, derived from the Hepplewhite and Sheraton types of the 1790s.

*c.1920*                                                       *£15 — £25*

# Bibliography

The reader who wishes to learn more about this very prolific and complex period will not be faced with all that great an availability of choice. The books listed below are some of the major ones concerned directly with furniture — reading on certain architects is also recommended. Otherwise, detailed research can be made from the Bibliography listed in Pauline Agius, p.186.

*British Furniture, 1880-1915*
 Pauline Agius, Woodbridge 1978
*The Pictorial Dictionary of British 19th Century Furniture Design*
 Antique Collectors' Club, Woodbridge 1977
*Victorian Furniture*
 R.W. Symonds and B.B. Whineray, London 1962
*19th Century Furniture*
 Elizabeth Aslin, 1962
'England 1830-1901' by Charles Handley Read in *World Furniture,*
 ed. Helena Hayward, 1965
*Victorian Furniture*
 Simon Jervis, 1968
*Charles Rennie Mackintosh, The Complete Furniture, etc.*
 Roger Billcliffe, 1979
*Modern English Furniture*
 J.C. Rogers, 1930
*The Adventure of British Furniture, 1851-1951*
 David Joel, London 1953
*Modern Cabinet Work*
 4th edition. Wells and Hooper, 1924
*Furniture for Small Houses*
 Percy A. Wells, London 1920